THE

Catholic

from the

Inside Out

Evangelizing the Culture
of Our Parish School

GARDEN & WALL

New York

To Sister Mary St. Lucian, B.V.M.

Garden & Wall publishes books on the philosophy and history of Catholic elementary education.

Copyright 2003 by Garden & Wall Educational Foundation P-101
ISBN 0-9727515-0-5
Library of Congress Catalog Control Number: 2002096803

Orders and information: Your bookseller, or Pathway Book Service, 4 White Brook Rd., Gilsum, NH 03448 TEL. 800-345-6665, FAX 603-357-2073. E-MAIL: pbs@pathwaybook.com

Contact us: Garden & Wall, 244 Fifth Ave L222, New York NY 10001. E-MAIL: gandw@att.net. WEB: gardenandwall.com

Contents

Preface

CATHOLIC ELEMENTARY SCHOOLS have a variety of purposes, and even those with identical goals may choose to pursue them in different ways. It is not our intention, therefore, to set forth principles and guidelines for all Catholic schools, or even to render a verdict on this or that theoretical approach to education.

Our principal aim is to add our voice to those who are calling for more support, encouragement, and training for lay teachers in our Catholic schools. In Chapter 17, we list three very specific needs that we cannot meet with local resources. Schools like ours need help from the wider Church.

A second aim is to tell our story. We studied the circumstances of our parish and locality; we looked into educational theory (some of it we liked, some of it we didn't); working from philosophy and theology, we clarified our school's nature, purpose and goals; we consulted widely; and we took some first, small steps toward evangelizing the culture of our school. Perhaps the story of our hopes and disappointments, our successes, and failures, will offer insight and encouragement to some who, like ourselves, are looking beyond educational methods and techniques to foundational principles, as they struggle to make their own school Catholic from the inside out.

We have chosen not to identify either the school that is the subject of this book, or the authors who wrote the report. We have made this choice not because of any desire for secrecy, but simply because we do not have the resources to respond to inquiries.

A few years ago, our principal attended the Elementary Principals Academy, sponsored by the National Catholic Educational Association. As part of that program, she committed herself to a field project in Catholic identity. She fulfilled this commitment through her leadership in the group effort described in this book.

During the four years that it took us to conceive and inaugurate the renewal in our school, we experienced the presence of the Holy Spirit, addressing our inadequacies and sustaining our vision. For us, this process was truly a spiritual journey.

Core Group
of the School Committee
of the Parish Advisory Council

1.

Where Angels Fear to Tread

CAN WE TAKE FULL ADVANTAGE of the opportunities our parish school offers? Can we evangelize its culture? Can we make it better and more truly Catholic, Catholic from the inside out?

When our Pastoral Council considered these questions several years ago, we were well aware that tinkering with schools is a risky business. Over the past hundred years education has become a professional field. Do non-professionals have anything worthwhile to say about a field where research and expertise play such a prominent part? Dare we enter in, where angels fear to tread?

With proper deference to those with professional expertise, we did dare to enter in. We did so because our school has other dimensions besides the professional. It has a pastoral dimension, since it is one of the ministries of our parish. It also has a parental   dimension,   because   parents   hold   ultimate responsibility for the education of their children.[1] The American bishops have clearly stated: "Catholic schools are called to a renewal of purpose."[2] As our school responded to the bishops' call to renewal, not only our professional educators, but our pastor, parishioners, and parents were very much involved.

Once we had made the decision to move ahead, here is what we did.

We set up a parish system of prayer. Although we planned to put our best work into this project, our ultimate trust was in God's help rather than our human efforts. For this reason we asked the sick, the shut-ins, and the entire parish to pray and sacrifice at every step of the way; we immersed the project in an ocean of prayer. There is no limit to the study and struggle that renewal can require. We knew we could not address all issues, but we gave of our best as time and circumstances allowed, leaving the rest in the hands of God.

We established channels of communication, so everyone would know what was going on. Channels included reports to the Pastoral Council, bulletins to parents and parish, and homilies on selected aspects of Catholic educational philosophy. In addition we wove informal community networks, at lunch counters and in beauty parlors. Loyal parishioners who made it their business to keep up with what was happening used these means to offer explanations, create positive attitudes, deflect criticism, and calm apprehensions. This communication played a major role in our eventual success.

We recruited a Core Group. We next invited all parishioners and people connected with the school to participate in the literature survey and reflection phases. Some did not believe themselves capable of dealing with so many abstract

---

[1] St. Thomas Aquinas, *Summa Theologica*, II-II, Q.102, Art.1; Pius XI, *On Christian Education* (1929), n. 32; Vatican II, *Declaration on Christian Education* (1965), n. 3.

[2] NCCB, *To Teach as Jesus Did* (USCC, 1972), n. 123.

ideas, but offered to help in practical ways later in the process. Others would have liked to participate, but did not have the time. Still others agreed to discuss specific points with us as the need arose. In the end we had five volunteers for the Core Group. There were two couples, each of whom had sent children through our school (one couple had sent eleven); and there was a parent of a current student. These volunteers, along with the pastor, the principal, and the parish provost, made up the Core Group.

We established contact with diocesan educational authorities. Our school is privileged to be part of a diocesan educational system that offers direction, inspiration, encouragement, and support. We worked within diocesan policies, keeping the authorities informed about what we were doing, welcoming their participation at whatever level they might desire. In this context we produced a document, *Statement of Principles,*[3] that indicated in a preliminary way how we intended to apply philosophical-theological principles to the various dimensions of our school. We sent our *Statement of Principles* to the diocesan education office. We received in response a letter of encouragement assuring us that what we were doing was "in conformity with diocesan educational philosophy". Having obtained this assurance, we were ready to begin.

We held meetings of parents in groups of twelve. We invited all parents to meet with the pastor and provost in a series of two-hour evening sessions, held in the living room of the Parish House. (At a later time, a similar meeting was held for teachers.) Fifty-two percent of our one hundred thirty school families elected to participate. Participants sat informally in a circle. During the first hour of each session, the pastor distributed and explained the *Statement of Principles* and answered questions. During the second hour, each participant in

---

[3] For our *Statement of Principles* see *Appendix D.*

turn had the opportunity to speak about the school: strengths, weaknesses, issues, suggestions. Our provost took notes, and later grouped the parents' comments into categories. As the study progressed, we made sure that all issues and suggestions were carefully considered.

At this time we made clear that we wanted to take full advantage of the wisdom that the Lord had placed in the minds and hearts of parents, teachers, students, parish leaders and parishioners. Although we did not intend to hold a lot of meetings, ideas were welcome at any time. Ideas came forth both in writing and informally in conversation. We received quite a few suggestions in this way, especially about practical ways of putting our principles into practice.[4]

Our Core Group reviewed the issues parents and others raised. After reviewing all submissions, we classified these ideas and suggestions into two categories: (1) those that relate to the teaching and learning process; and (2) those that relate to the setting of the school.

We studied the history of American education, especially to learn how certain aspects of progressivism became part of the popular concept of the elementary school. We are an American school. Whether we agreed or not with specific aspects of the dominant educational philosophy, we needed to become familiar with that philosophy before we laid out our own school's statement of nature, purpose and goals.[5] One reason for this

---

[4] Notable among them was a parent's suggestion that we speak of repentance instead of discipline in our school.

[5] We knew we could not read everything we might want to read on education, so we prepared a list of categories, intending to survey at least something in each of the following topics: history of elementary education in the United States; the works of John Dewey; anthologies of important American educational writing; introductory texts for teacher training; modern developmental psychology; texts on current motivational systems; educational testing; technology; recent works on American educational philosophy; literature offering a critique of current educational theory and practice; selected Catholic authors on educational philosophy; church documents and treatises on religious education; materials from the National Catholic Educational Association,

study was that we might benefit from the valid educational insights that developed from the progressive system. Another reason was cultural. Since progressive educational theory and practice tend to define education for Americans, including Catholics, we wanted to understand better the cultural assumptions and expectations our parents had, as they brought their children to our school.

We looked at the circumstances of our parish and school. Our situation places boundaries, and to some extent limitations, on what our school is able to do. Further, Catholic schools are not all alike. We assume that our school differs in certain ways from others, because our circumstances are different.

We stated our school's nature, context, ultimate purpose and goals. We made this statement in the light of Catholic theology,[6] the circumstances affecting the way our school operates, educational theory, and, to some extent, insights from parents and others. We wanted the purpose of our school to come into sharp focus.[7]

We then studied the issues, and decided what approach we would take to confront each category. In the first category (teaching and learning), we chose to consider verbal skills and

including the journal, *Momentum*; and *Catholic Education: A Journal of Inquiry and Practice.*

[6] We found the following works especially helpful as background for reflecting on our school's purpose: Harold A. Buetow, *The Catholic School: Its Roots, Identity, and Future* (Crossroads, 1988), and *Of Singular Benefit: The Story of Catholic Education in the United States* (Macmillan, 1970); William F. Cunningham, *The Pivotal Problems of Education: An Introduction to the Christian Philosophy of Education* (Macmillan, 1940); Jacques Maritain, *Education at the Crossroads* (Yale University Press, 1943); Bernard Lonergan, *Topics in Education*, vol. 10 of *The Collected Works of Bernard Lonergan* (University of Toronto Press, 1988); Edward A. Fitzpatrick, *The Philosophy of Education* (Bruce, 1953); Edward Leen, *What Is Education?* (Sheed & Ward, 1944). We also consulted a recent work: James T. Byrnes, *John Paul II & Educating for Life* (Peter Lang, 2002).

[7] Maritain warns of the danger of concentrating on educational methods without careful consideration of purposes. He says that a fixation on methods can result in a psychological worship of the child. Maritain, *Crossroads*, p. 17.

religion. In the second category (school setting), we chose the following: the teacher; student motivation; joy in school life; repentance (discipline); Catholic experiences; manners for children, teachers, and parents; the school's physical environment; trust in God as a basis for policy-making. Wrestling with these topics in prayer and deciding what to do was the heart of the process.

We held a three-day teacher seminar. The purpose of this seminar was to assess our teachers' understanding of the proposed changes, and to gauge their willingness to move ahead. Our teachers, all very loyal and devout lay persons, were most supportive of the entire undertaking. Because their college training had largely imposed a progressive education orientation, however, teachers found it difficult at first to understand what we were saying about Christian versus behaviorist motivation, and about non-experiential approaches to teaching. It took some time, but teachers made splendid adjustments in style and approach when the implementation actually began.

We rewrote our School Handbook. We prepared a new edition of our *Handbook*, incorporating the results of our studies and deliberations. In the new edition, we provided a detailed explanation of our philosophy, as well as a description of the policies, procedures and expectations that would apply when changes came at the beginning of the next school year. We sent the *Handbook* to the diocese and to all parents for comment. We invited people to contact us with any questions, observations, or difficulties. Unhappily, we received almost no response, one way or another. Since there seemed to be no objection, however, we finalized the text of the *Handbook* and had it printed.

We made the Core Group the School Committee of the Pastoral Council. We also enlarged the committee to include two parents who had expressed deep interest during the planning stage, who were willing to do serious reading and critical thinking.

We inaugurated the new era. After two years of planning, we were now ready to move into implementation. We projected many changes in our school, some of them quite extensive. As part of the re-registration process for the upcoming year, we asked all parents to state in writing that they had studied the *Handbook*, and that they were prepared to accept its provisions. An intense period of prayer accompanied this step. We asked parents of new students to come to a four-hour orientation session, conducted by members of the Core Group. During this session, the Core Group explained the *Handbook* and answered questions. Afterward, those parents who wished their children to enter our school signed a *Memorandum of Agreement*[8] and were permitted to apply. Not all parents opted to apply, but most did.

The first year was not without excitement. Crises abounded. The story of what happened is related in Chapters 5 and following.

---

[8] For the text of this memorandum see p. 89.

2.

A Catholic School is Different.
From What?

Public School Progressive Education

Here's what we discovered when we looked into the development of American elementary education.[1]

By 1860, most states had established public school systems, under the relentless hammering of Horace Mann[2] and others, who had by that time convinced the American people that common schools were essential to national progress. Common schools--free of charge, universally available, and public--would provide the knowledge needed for citizens of a democracy to make intelligent decisions, and, through the warmth of childhood associations, would create a nation of people living in social harmony.[3]

---

[1] We found Lawrence A. Cremin's *The Transformation of the School* (Knopf, 1964) very helpful for understanding how the American school evolved. Diane Ravitch's *Left Behind: A Century of Battles Over School* Reform (Simon & Schuster, 2000) brings the story up to date. Also useful was the text by Adrian M. Dupuis and Robin L. Gordon, *Philosophy of Education in Historical Perspective*, second edition (University Press of America, 1977). Neil G. McCluskey's *Catholic Viewpoint on Education* (Image Books, 1962), pp. 40-56, supplied a Catholic perspective.

[2] Horace Mann (1796-1859) was Secretary of the Massachusetts Board of Education and an outstanding promoter of the public school system.

It was W. T. Harris of St. Louis who ultimately rationalized the institution of the public school. Harris was a speculative philosopher (a Hegelian), a dynamic speaker, and an energetic administrator. As superintendent of St. Louis schools (1868-1880), and as U.S. Commissioner of Education (1889-1909), he fully supported the ideals of Horace Mann. His contribution was to promote the idea of formal order in American schools. He introduced the graded school, stressed hard work, insisted on the teaching of fundamentals in elementary schools, promoted teacher training and adequate compensation, introduced classroom supervision, and advocated well-designed school buildings. He also sought to limit schooling to what children are not likely to learn from family, church, and community. For Harris, the primary purpose of the public school was to train the mind and to provide mental discipline, so that children will be competent to make democracy work.[4]

Yet, even during Harris' lifetime, forces at work in American society pushed to expand the scope of the common school. The need to improve the lives of poor immigrants, along with the need to encourage young people to stay on the farms, fueled the demand for job training.

The last quarter of the nineteenth century introduced manual training, especially into secondary schools. The movement developed to such an extent that by 1910 vocational courses and schools had become primary sources of training in agriculture, technology, trade, home economics, and industrial arts. By 1917, the passage of the Smith-Hughes Act had confirmed the U.S. government's financial and moral support of this development.[5]

---

[3] Cremin, *Transformation*, pp. 8-14.

[4] *Ibid.*, pp. 14-20.

[5] Inspired by the work of Victor Della Vos, director of the Moscow Imperial Technical School, John D. Runkle, president of M.I.T., and Calvin M. Woodward, of Washington University, St. Louis, began to promote manual training as part of liberal education for all schools. W. T. Harris attacked the concept as subversive, but popular sentiment was so favorable that the ideal of manual arts as part of liberal education gave way to the ideal of manual arts for the sake of job training. In some schools, especially those above the elementary level, liberal arts disappeared altogether. It is interesting to note that forty

In the meantime, Jane Addams[6] and her co-workers were attempting to address the plight of poor immigrants through the Settlement House Movement. The movement aimed to promote the reestablishment of a sense of community in the urban slums, crowded by large numbers of European immigrants and by rural migrants in search of city jobs. Although the settlement houses themselves provided a wide range of social services, their enduring significance was their impact on the American school. The Settlement House leadership protested vigorously against a restricted view of the school. The movement, impatient with the stress on reading and writing, as though all knowledge must be brought to children through the medium of books, was outspoken in advocating a more child-centered curriculum. Education of the handicapped, school lunches, libraries, child care, home economics, art and music, physical education and hygiene, adult education, kindergartens, smaller classes, improved buildings, and better teachers—all these innovations came from the settlement houses. As a result, the movement contributed substantially to expanding the definition of the common schools to include remedies for social problems.[7]

However distressing their slums, the cities of the nineteenth century continued to call young people who wished to escape the loneliness and poverty of the farms. Liberty Hyde Bailey of Cornell, along with colleagues in what came to be known as the Country Life Movement, promoted nature study as the great remedy for alienation of people from the land. Thus the study of rural naturalness, simplicity of living and sympathy with common things became a major emphasis in rural schools, further enlarging the scope of schools in the direction of solving social problems.[8]

---

years later American industry faced a crisis after World War II, and had to re-emphasize its own apprenticeship programs. *Ibid.*, p. 57.

[6] Jane Addams (1860-1935), a social reformer, was founder of Hull House in Chicago, and a leader in the Settlement House Movement.

[7] Cremin, *Transformation*, pp. 58-74.

[8] *Ibid.*, pp. 75-85.

By 1900, an educational revolution was at hand.[9] Not only did the promoters of every civic cause have their program for the school, but theories and ideas, old and new, abounded. For example: children have stages of development (Jan Komensky); empiricism as a philosophy of education (John Locke); permissive learning (Jean-Jacques Rousseau); object lessons (Johann Pestalozzi); each subject should be taught in relation to other subjects (Johan Herbart); early childhood stimulation (Maria Montessori); the kindergarten (Friedrich Froebel); the preeminence of science (Herbert Spencer); Social Darwinism (William Sumner, Lester Ward, Albion Small); child-centered education (Theodore Parker); child development (Stanley Hall); educational psychology (William James); and quantifiable testing (Edward Thorndike).[10]

It was John Dewey (1859-1952), however, who first proposed a comprehensive theory underlying what came to be called progressive education. Dewey asked himself what kind of schools a democracy such as America needed.[11] His answer was that the nation could best be served by an educational system focused not so much on abstract subject matter, but on the experience of life. He explained his theory in *Democracy and*

---

[9]   The spark that set off the revolution might well have been the muckraking series of articles based on a tour of the nation, published in *The Forum* in the 1890s, by Joseph Mayer Rice. Rice found that time after time, politicians were hiring untrained teachers who led their pupils in singsong drill and rote repetition. Only at Francis Parker's school in Chicago did he find an example of the well-rounded education of children, including nature study, social activities and art as well as the three R's, all taught by competent and enthusiastic teachers. *Ibid.*, pp. 3-8.

[10]   We found a good summary of pre-Dewey educational theories in Allan Orstein and Daniel Levine, *Foundations of Education*, sixth ed. (Houghton Mifflin, 1977), pp. 101-110.

[11]   Dewey was in the tradition of Horace Mann and W. T. Harris, who both believed that common schools were necessary for democracy. His experiential approach to education, however, was in sharp disagreement with the formal approach advocated by W. T. Harris, and was in many ways in reaction to it.

Education,[12] a classic work, on sale to this day in bookstores of colleges that offer teaching degrees.[13]

Dewey was essentially a philosopher. Along with William James and C. S. Pierce he is a founder of the American philosophy called pragmatism. According to pragmatism, truth is what works. *It is the very nature of thought to be ordered to practical action*.[14] True knowledge *is doing* rather than merely *seeing*. Truth (including values) can be affirmed only through the experiential[15] method. When a problem or issue arises, the mind first proposes a hypothesis, and then tests the hypothesis by observation based on the individual's own experience or that of others. If careful testing reveals the consequences to be favorable, not just for the individual but for the common good, the hypothesis is true. Thus the truth of the last seven Commandments can be established because these Commandments actually work to facilitate a good society. According to Dewey, the truth of the first three Commandments cannot be established because there is no way of proving the existence of a Supreme Being. Teaching about God, and therefore about supernatural and revealed religion, is not truly educative.[16]

Dewey's religious views are instructive.[17] He affirmed the need for religion to provide joy, consolation, strength, and

---

[12]   John Dewey, *Democracy and Education: An Introduction to the Philosophy of Education*, first published 1916 (Free Press, 1966).

[13]   Among John Dewey's other important educational works are: *Experience and Education*, first published 1938 (Simon & Schuster, 1997); *The School and Society and The Child and the Curriculum*, first published 1900 (University of Chicago, 1990); *Moral Principles in Education*, first published 1909 (Southern Illinois University Press, 1975).

[14]   "Problems of Men and the Present State of Philosophy", and "Value and Thought", in Dewey, *Problems of Men* (New York. Philosophical Library, 1946).

[15]   Pragmatists do not limit experimentation to the strictly scientific, but also include the type of careful experimentation the ordinary person undertakes in everyday life.

[16]   Frederick Coppleston, *A History Of Philosophy*, vol. 8:2, pp. 109 ff., helped us better to understand Dewey's philosophy of naturalistic empiricism and his concept of truth. McCluskey discusses Dewey's religious views at length in *Catholic Viewpoint*, Chapter 3.

inspiration, but held that traditional supernatural religion based
on the concept of God and the afterlife has become unbelievable
since it comprises a set of symbols that today are empty of meaning. In his view, we must keep the schools free from this bias.
We must pull down the old barns, and work hard to place in the
school religious feelings and religious thoughts, a positive creed
of life consistent with modern democracy and modern science.[18]
Here are Dewey's own words:

> So far as education is concerned, those who
> believe in religion as a natural expression
> of human experience must devote themselves
> to the development of the ideas of life which
> lie implicit in our still new science and our
> still newer democracy. They must interest
> themselves in the transformation of those
> institutions which still bear the dogmatic and
> the feudal stamp till they are in accord with
> these ideas. In performing this service, it
> is their business to do what they can to prevent
> all public educational agencies from being employed
> in ways which inevitably impede the recognition of
> the spiritual import of science and of democracy,
> and hence of that type of religion which will be
> the fine flower of the modern spirit's achievement.[19]

---

[17]   The thirty-one principal places where Dewey treated the subject of religion are listed
and discussed in Horace L. Freiss, "Dewey's Philosophy of Religion", in Jo Ann
Boytdston, ed., *Guide to the Works of John Dewey* (Southern Illinois University Press,
1970), pp. 200-217.

[18]   Dewey, "Religion and Our Schools", *Hibbert Journal*, VI (July, 1908), 796-809.

[19]   Dewey, *Hibbert Journal*, VI, 808-809. Another important statement is found in
Dewey's *Human Nature and Conduct: An Introduction to Social Psychology*, first
published 1922 (Modern Library, 1957), pp. 330-331.

Reflecting on Dewey's position, our Core Group concluded that Dewey's goal of placing a creed compatible with democracy and science at the center of the public school system has only too well been accomplished. It would be interesting if someone made a study of the "positive creed of life" assumed or taught in public schools. Such a study would confirm our hypothesis that in America the public school has become the established religion.

In line with his pragmatic philosophy, Dewey defined education as "...that reconstruction or reorganization of experience which adds to the meaning of experience, and which increases the ability to direct the course of subsequent experience."[20] He proposed guidelines for teachers: Begin with the experience and interests of the child. Connect what he learns to all of life. Serve as a non-authoritarian guide. Help children discover meaning in their experience, by testing the consequences, through their own careful observations and those of others, including classmates and teachers. Give students the experience of problem-solving in the classroom community, not just as a preparation for adult life, but as part of life here and now. Assist children in organizing their experience so that they will end up with a systematic knowledge of subject matter. That way, children will *grow* in their ability to solve practical problems as members of a democracy. The image is that of the scoutmaster leading his charges through familiar territory, and helping them work together to discover meaning: that is, to solve practical problems. The scoutmaster has a more advanced and systematic knowledge of what he intends to teach, but he wants the children to experience the thrill of discovery. Ideally they too should end up with systematic, practical knowledge.

All of life contains meaning; schooling, therefore, should not be limited to the traditional subjects. The experiential approach, applied to a broad range of subjects, will prepare children to be life-long learners.

---

[20] Dewey, *Democracy and Education*, p. 76.

Like many of his contemporaries, Dewey was in reaction against uninspired methods of teaching, especially rote memorization, recitation and drill. The new education stressed the active cooperation of the child, rather than information imposed from above; freedom rather than repression; the teacher as guide rather than as an authoritarian figure; learning by doing rather than from teachers and textbooks; setting appealing goals for children instead of inculcating skills by drill; making the most of the present instead of preparing only for the child's adult future; equipping children to meet the challenges of a changing world, instead of cramming static subject-matter into their heads. Dewey was particularly disdainful of memorization and drill, techniques he claimed "dulled the powers of judgment, induced boredom and drudgery, and [were] not relevant to anything outside the school."[21]

In 1938, Dewey gave a series of lectures, later published under the title *Experience and Education*.[22] In these lectures he restated his educational theory in the context of the difficulties, criticisms and misrepresentations that had arisen over the past twenty years. In this book of lectures we encountered the complexity of his thought: here, as elsewhere, Dewey did not always express himself clearly. We struggled to understand his point of view, however, and summarized it for ourselves in ten statements:

1. All genuine education comes through experience. But the experience has to be the right kind.

2. Truly educational experience promotes worthwhile future experiences and influences growth.

3. The school is a social setting where students, cooperating with others in problem-

---

[21]   Dewey, *Experience and Education*, pp. 18, 19, 27, 34; Dewey, *Democracy and Education*, pp. 186, 187, 192.

[22]   Reprinted by Simon & Schuster, 1997.

solving, learn not only principles of morality, but moral attitudes, actions, and habits.

4. In guiding the student, the teacher calls on the wisdom of wider experience to direct the child's experience (1) in continuity with previous experience, and (2) in interaction[23] with the child's present surroundings. This approach develops habits of thinking that employ past and present experiences so as to promote future growth.

5. Physical ordering of the classroom restricts the child's ability to learn. The classroom should possess a climate of freedom where pupils rarely need direct control. Chaos, however, is not desirable. Having rules of the game is not a restriction on freedom.

6. When the teacher fails to enlist the cooperation of the student, learning does not occur.

7. Learning begins with impulse or desire; continues with careful observation and reflection on personal experience and that of others with wider experience; and proceeds to judgment about the impulse's meaning, significance, consequences. This process transforms an impulse into a "purpose". In giving guidance, teachers should avoid forcing the young into channels that lead toward the teacher's purpose rather than the student's.

8. Purpose translates into a plan of action through selection of means (analysis) and arrangement of means to reach the purpose (synthesis). This process first states a hypothesis and then tests the hypothesis by careful observation of the consequences. Such

---

[23] Field trips would be an example of interaction with the child's surroundings.

testing, done correctly, achieves truth, and education occurs. Truth is what works.

9. By keeping track of ideas, activities and observed consequences, children learn to review, summarize and record their experience under the teacher's guidance, adding facts, information, and ideas to their expanding world of organized subject matter. This accomplishment is "growth".

10. It is much more difficult to teach experientially than to employ the traditional method. The teacher must become aware of each individual's particular needs and capacities, and must provide the conditions that enable the content of experiences to satisfy those needs and develop those capacities. Truly educational experiences do not repel the child, but engage his interest and active participation.

In the closing pages of *Experience and Education*,[24] Dewey complained about educators who supposedly adopted his methods but failed in practice to achieve tangible results. In his response to the criticism that his practices were far too demanding for the average teacher, Dewey advised these educators simply to work harder, because his method is necessarily more difficult for the teacher than the older methods.[25]

Dewey's ideas exerted enormous influence because he tried to show the relevance of education to everyday life, because he placed new emphasis on the child to be taught, because he advocated humane methods of teaching to arouse the child's interest, and because he struck the chord of practicality in the American temperament.

---

[24] Dewey, *Experience and Education*, p. 90.

[25] We found this criticism expressed in Philip Jackson's introduction to the University of Chicago's 1990 edition of Dewey's *The School and Society*, p. xi.

Dewey's convoluted language was difficult for teachers and others not philosophically inclined to understand, however. William H. Kilpatrick, Dewey's student and a professor at Teachers College in New York, became the universal exponent and interpreter of his teacher's ideas.

Like Dewey, Kilpatrick believed in experiential learning, and, in 1918, he employed the term "project method" to make the concept more readily understandable. For Kilpatrick, a project is "a wholehearted purposeful activity". Here is an example: "Imagine a boy at home making a wireless outfit.... He starts out, meets a difficulty, studies the books and all the apparatus he can see, finds out where his difficulty lies, and remedies that. This done, he starts again, after awhile meets a new difficulty, again studies, again succeeds in overcoming the difficulty. And so on through the whole thing. In the end he can hear distant stations."[26]

Kilpatrick visualized a succession of large projects to replace the traditional approach to subject matter. "As I see it," he said, "our schools have in the past chosen from the whole of life certain intellectualist tools..., have arranged these under the heads of reading, arithmetic, geography, and so on, and have taught these separately as if they would, when once acquired, recombine into the worthy life."[27]

Dewey believed Kilpatrick's project method to be generally compatible with his own theory, even though he differed with Kilpatrick in one important respect. Dewey visualized the teacher, through experiential learning, assisting students in acquiring systematic knowledge of subject matter, (although it was not exactly clear from his writings just how this systematization was to come about). Kilpatrick, on the other hand, saw little need for systematic knowledge. He conducted an unrelenting attack on pre-selected subject matter.[28] For

---

[26] William H. Kilpatrick, *Foundations of Method* (Macmillan, 1925), p. 284. Kilpatrick's theory was originally published in an article entitled, "The Project Method", *Teachers College Record*, XIX: 4 (September, 1918), 319-335.

[27] Kilpatrick, *Foundations*, p. 108.

Kilpatrick it was not knowledge but "learning how to learn" that was all-important. Schools should teach children *how* to think, not *what* to think; methods of *seeking* truth, rather than *truth itself.*[29]

Dewey was uncomfortable with that viewpoint. For the rest of his career, Dewey argued a point he never fully communicated to his disciples: a teacher cannot take advantage of experiential teaching opportunities without a clear sense of what is to come later. What is to come later is organized knowledge as contained in the disciplines.[30] In trying to make Dewey's theories available for popular use, Kilpatrick managed to transpose them into something quite different.[31]

From 1918 to 1928 Kilpatrick taught 35,000 student teachers. Thus Dewey's theory of progressive education, revised by Kilpatrick, became, and still remains, the most characteristic element of a public school movement that redefined education in terms of process rather than knowledge.[32]

Another prominent progressive theme in the 1920s was an increased emphasis on the child-centered versus the subject-centered school.[33] By 1926, Dewey himself was becoming a critic of exaggerations in the practices of some of his disciples. Expressing a negative view of the deliberate downplaying of adult guidance in some child-centered schools, he called the

---

[28] Cremin, *Transformation*, p. 218.

[29] What *we* think about Kilpatrick's emphasis for elementary age children will be treated in the chapter to follow.

[30] Cremin, *Transformation*, p. 138.

[31] Cremin, *Transformation*, p. 221.

[32] *Ibid.*, p. 221. We also consulted Charles A. McMurry, *Teaching by Projects* (Macmillan, 1920).

[33] "Child-centered" could have a variety of meanings: a curriculum related to life; active participation of children in learning; teaching based on internal motivation rather than external inducements; more attention to children's developmental stages; building on children's interests; greater effort to promote self-esteem and to create a sense of self-fulfillment. A classic work on this development is: Harold Rugg and Ann Shumaker, *The Child-Centered School* (Arno Press, 1969).

practice stupid. "Baby," Dewey insisted, "does not know best".[34]

By the beginning of World War II, thousands of local school districts had adopted one or another element of the progressive approach: expanded curriculum, such as manual training, home economics, and nature study; grouping students by ability based on testing; teaching aids, such as colorful text-books, visuals; field trips; the project method; greater awareness of child-development; less authoritative teachers, and concern for the child's health, self-image and life adjustment; extra-curricular activities brought into the curriculum; school-sponsored community service; more elaborate physical plants: gyms, pools, shops, cafeterias, playgrounds; movable seats in classrooms; junior high schools.[35]

A 1940 Gallup poll indicated that public opinion generally favored what was going on in the schools. By 1944, however, the National Opinion Research Center reported that forty-four percent of people responding desired modifications in educational methods in directions decidedly unprogressive. Long-smoldering criticisms of progressive education suddenly erupted. Bernard Bell's 1949 book, *Crisis in Education*,[36] for example, blamed progressivism for the unsatisfactory state of our life and culture. The elementary schools had failed to transmit the wisdom of the race, were coddling students, had been systematically divested of intellectual content, had taken over parental functions.

The criticisms by Bell and others, combined with the Sputnik crisis, produced a brief return to basics and knowledge-oriented education in the 1950s. But the upheavals of the 1960s brought a relapse into progressivism, this time with a heavy

---

[34] Dewey, *Art and Education*, third edition (Barnes Foundation, 1954).

[35] *Time Magazine* (October 31, 1938) stated that progressivism was no longer a rebel movement, but was mainstream and respectable. Cited in Cremin, *Transformation*, p. 324.

[36] Bernard Iddings Bell, *Crisis in Education: A Challenge to American Complacency* (Whittlesey House, 1949).

emphasis on education as therapy.[37]   Self-image, attention to feelings, self-esteem, and child-centeredness came into a prominence that remains to this day.

From the 1960s to the present, there has been a virtual chorus of complaint, typified by the publication of *A Nation at Risk* in 1983 by the National Commission on Excellence in Education.[38] Today the shelves of bookstores are replete with proposals for reform from every conceivable direction.[39] Education has become a prominent issue in the political arena.

Still, there is no doubt that John Dewey's theories have had their impact, and continue to have significant influence on American education to this day.[40] In his lifetime, Dewey wrote

---

[37]   Maureen Stout, *The Feel-Good Curriculum: The Dumbing-Down of America's Kids in the Name of Self-Esteem* (Perseus, 2000).

[38]   *A Nation at Risk*, (U.S. Department of Education, 1983).

[39]   Some of the current and older reformist books that we perused: E. D. Hirsch, *The Schools We Need and Why We Don't Have Them* (Doubleday, 1996); Robert M. Hutchins, *The Conflict in Education in a Democratic Society* (Harper, 1953); Mortimer Smith, *And Madly Teach* (Regnery, 1949); Arthur E. Bestor, *Educational Wastelands: The Retreat from Learning in Our Public Schools* (University of Illinois, 1953); Boyd H. Bode, *Progressive Education at the* Crossroads (Newsom, 1938); I. L. Kandel, *The Cult of Uncertainty* (Macmillan, 1943); Michael Demiashkevich, *An Introduction to the Philosophy of Education* (American Books, 1935); William Begley, *Education and Emergent Man* (Nelson, 1934); Hyman Rickover, *Education and Freedom* (Dutton, 1959); Allan Bloom, *The Closing of the American Mind* (Simon & Schuster, 1987); Helen F. Ladd, ed., *Holding Schools Accountable* (Brookings, 1996); Anne Husted Burleigh, *Education in a Free* Society (Liberty, 1973); Martin L. Gross, *The Conspiracy of Ignorance: The Failure of American Public Schools* (Harper Collins, 1999); William J. Bennett, Chester E. Finn, and John T. E. Cribb, *The Educated Child* (Simon & Schuster, 1999); John T. Gatto, *The Underground History of American Education: A Schoolteacher's Intimate Investigation into the Problem of Modern Schooling* (Oxford Village Press, 2000); Gene E. Veith and Andrew Kern, *Classical Education: Towards the Revival of American Schooling* (Capital Research, 1997); David C. Paris, *Ideology and Educational Reform: Themes and Theories in Public Education* (Westview, 1995). Hancock offers a reason why many modern proposals for reform are incomplete—such proposals neglect to integrate into their solutions a theological-philosophical view of the nature and destiny of human beings. Curtis L. Hancock, in Peter A. Redpath, ed., *From Twilight to Dawn: The Cultural Vision of Jacques Maritain* (American Maritain Association, 1990), pp. 241-260.

[40]   Lonergan, *Topics in Education*, p. 4. Dewey's impact was brought home to us in the description Fishman and McCarthy gave of their experience at Columbia University and the University of Chicago. In their student days Dewey was no longer the direct focus of the curriculum, but Fishman and McCarthy realized that through a tacit tradition, Dewey

dozens of books and articles. In his writings, Dewey expounded his concept of the human person, his view of the pragmatic nature of truth and goodness, and his understanding of the process of knowing. He then discussed how to employ principles from his pragmatic philosophy in defining the purpose of the school, in motivating students, in deciding what is to be taught in the school, in establishing teaching methods, in describing the qualities of the ideal teacher, in determining classroom environment, and in fostering the proper relationship between the school and the community. Dewey produced the first comprehensive, systematic treatment of the philosophy of education in modern times.[41]

Where are we today? In search of answers to this question, we surveyed several recent works on educational theory.[42] Some authors called strongly for a renewed interest in philosophy.[43]

---

was "everywhere in our work". Stephen Fishman and Lucille McCarthy, *John Dewey and the Challenge of Classroom Practice* (Columbia University Teachers College, 1998), p. 11. Flusche states: "Pragmatism as advanced by Dewey and followers has become part of the moral, religious, legal, business and educational thinking of this country." Ernest Flusche, *A Critical Study of Current Concepts of Truth in American Educational Theory and Their Educational Implications* (Catholic University Press, 1961), p. 17.

[41] Dupuis, *Philosophy of Education*, p. 1. Different authors employ he term "philosophy of education" in different ways, as Ellis A. Joseph explains in Thomas C. Hunt *et al.*, eds., *Handbook of Research on Catholic Education* (Greenwood, 2001), pp. 27-35. In this book we use the term to denote the ultimate principles constituting the basis of education. In referring to the educational philosophy of our school, we mean the ultimate philosophical-theological principles whereon our school is founded. For us, Catholic philosophy refers to Thomism, and theological principles refer to the teaching of the Church. We understand the relationship between philosophy and theology to be that described by John Paul II in the encyclical *Fides et Ratio* (September 1, 1998). The focus of our interest in Catholic philosophy of education is the nature of truth and morality, the nature and destiny of human beings, how people acquire knowledge, and ultimate purposes and goals of various types of Catholic elementary schools.

[42] Christopher Winch and John Gingell, *Key Concepts in the Philosophy of Education* (Routledge, 1999); Nigel Blake *et al.*, *Thinking Again: Education after Postmodernism* (Bergin & Garvey, 1998); Robert Heslep, *Philosophical Thinking in Educational Practice* (Praeger, 1997); Wendy Kohli, ed., *Critical Conversations in Philosophy of Education* (Indiana University Press, 1995); Larry A. Hickman, ed., *Reading Dewey: Interpretations for a Postmodern Generation*, (Indiana University Press, 1998); George R. Knight, *Issues and Alternatives in Educational Philosophy* (Andrews University, 1989); Kathe Jervis and Carol Montag, eds., *Progressive Education for the 1990s: Transforming Practice* (Teachers College Press, 1991); Howard Ozmon and Samuel Craver, *Philosophical Foundations of Education* (Merrill, 1981).

Others were content to write about teaching methods, child psychology, and administration. The dozen or so teacher-training programs that we reviewed were heavy with courses in pedagogy, psychology, and educational administration. When we looked for philosophy, we were referred to courses entitled "Fundamentals of Education". Upon examination, the student-texts employed in these courses described a variety of philosophical approaches to education, followed by an exhortation to the students to "choose your own philosophy," and "seek to be employed by a school with whose philosophy you agree."[44]

Thinking about all these ideas and reviewing all this history created a strong desire in our Core Group to define our school with as much precision as possible. The public school furnishes our culture with an image of what an elementary school is supposed to be. Although this image contains variations, certain core ideas arouse expectations in the minds of the parents who choose to send their children to our school. In fairness to our parents, to their children, and to ourselves, it seemed critically important to set forth as clearly as possible the philosophical and theological principles upon which our school's purpose, nature, and educational approach ultimately rest.[45]

---

[43]   Among these authors are: Paris, *Ideology and Educational Reform;* Neil Postman, *The End of Education: Redefining the Value of School* (Vintage, 1996); Knight, *Issues and Alternatives;* Veith, *Classical Education.*

[44]   We found the same texts being used in both Catholic and in state colleges: Ornstein, *Foundations of Education;* Robert F. McNergney, *Foundations of Education: The Challenge of Professional Practice,* third edition (Allyn & Bacon, 2000); James A. Johnson, *Introduction to the Foundations of American Education,* twelfth edition (Allyn & Bacon, 2001).

[45]   As early as 1932, George Johnson urged Catholic schools to develop a working philosophy of education that defined principles and would "enable us to break the fetters of imitation and conformity". George Johnson, "The Need for a Catholic Philosophy of Education", in Charles A. Hart, ed., *Aspects of the New Scholastic Philosophy* (Benziger, 1932), p. 303.

3.

Some Things We Like—
Some We Don't

Our Response to the Progressives

OUR CORE GROUP DID NOT PROPOSE to deliver a systematic critique of pragmatism and the other philosophies that permeate American public education. Others have done so, and we are grateful for their insights.[1] Instead, we offer the results of our discussions, in which we struggled to understand the Thomistic approach to education, against the background of what we had learned about the public school. Later we will explain how we applied the insights we obtained to the everyday life of our school.

---

[1] Buetow, *Catholic School*, pp. 26-46; Flusche, *Critical Study*; Maritain, *Crossroads*, pp. 1-28, 103-118; Cunningham, *Pivotal Problems*, pp. 25-54; Donald De Marco, "The Darkening of the Intellect: Four Ways of Sinning against the Light", in Daniel McInerny, ed., *The Common Things: Essays on Thomism and Education* (American Maritain Association, 1999); Curtis L. Hancock, "A Return to the Crossroads: A Maritain View of the New Educational Reformers", in Peter A. Redpath, ed., *From Twilight to Dawn: The Cultural Vision of Jacques Maritain* (Notre Dame Press, 1990); Jude P. Dougherty, *Recent American Naturalism: An Exposition and Critique* (Catholic University Press, 1960).

Truth. The pragmatic idea of truth as "that which works" is too narrow and restrictive for us, for two reasons. First, such a definition would relegate to the realm of mere opinion anything-- such as the existence of God--that empirical observation cannot verify.[2] Second, the pragmatic concept of truth excludes the possibility divine revelation. The basic philosophical tenet at the heart of progressive education, therefore, is directly contrary to what we hold and believe.

As Thomists,[3] our Core Group embraces the concept of the intrinsic value of truth, defined as "conformity of the mind to reality". It is not just our *ideas* that we know, but we know *things themselves*. Things exist outside our minds, entirely apart from whether we know them or not. If there is correspondence between our minds and what is out there in reality, we have achieved truth. If not, we are in error, however sincere we might be.

We bring our minds into contact with reality in a variety of ways, not just through the type of experience Dewey described. Among these ways of contacting reality are abstraction, induction, deduction, synthesis, and reflection. Each of these paths, rightly followed, can lead to truth.

We do not share the pessimism of those who believe that human beings are incapable of reaching certainty about anything. Every affirmation is not an hypothesis; the human mind can embrace the truth. Since our minds are finite, however, our knowledge is limited. We are incapable of knowing everything about even the smallest atom; we can always learn more.

The Thomistic theory of knowledge is called "modified realism". It is called realism because what we know is something that really exists outside the mind. It is called

---

[2] Dougherty, *American Naturalism*, pp. 20 ff.

[3] Two authors guided us to the places where St. Thomas Aquinas treated the topics discussed in this chapter. The locations include: *Summa Theologica, De Veritate* (including *De Magistro*), *Summa Contra Gentiles, Quaestiones Disputatae, Quodlibeta*. The two authors are: Mary Helen Mayer, *The Philosophy of Teaching of St. Thomas Aquinas* (Bruce, 1928); and Pierre H. Conway, *Principles of Education: a Thomistic Approach* (Thomist Press, 1960). We found a good summary of the Aristotelian-Thomistic theory of knowledge in Coppleston, *History of Philosophy*, vol. 2:2, pp. 108-117.

modified because the finite nature of our minds always limits our knowledge. Modified realism is the philosophical foundation of the approach to teaching in our school. We believe that truth, defined in this way, may be both learned and taught.

Moral Goodness. We are also uncomfortable with Dewey's pragmatic idea of moral goodness. He described good actions as those whose consequences have been judged good for, and by, society at a particular time and place.[4] For us, the end (consequence) does not justify the means. We are at one with Pope John Paul II, who in *Veritatis Splendor*[5] strongly reaffirmed Catholic teaching on the objective nature of moral truth. Known by reason and revelation, objective morality is set forth in the teaching of the Church.

We are well aware that the pragmatic definition of morality is deeply embedded in American culture.[6] Our attempt to teach objective morality is one of the most prominent counter-cultural characteristics of our school.

Human Beings and Their Destiny. Progressives deny that humans are created by a Supreme Being, but believe that they evolved on their own power from lower species and are still evolving. Environment, social context, and education largely determine how people act; free will does not enter in. People are to seek the fulfillment of their ultimate destiny in this life rather than in the life to come.[7]

As Catholics, we know from both reason and revelation that human beings are created by God. Their bodies may have evolved from lower species through God's power, but their

---

[4]   Dewey, *Experience and Education*, Chapter 26; and *Moral Principles in Education*, Chapter 4.

[5]   John Paul II, *Veritatis Splendor*, (August 6, 1993).

[6]   Dupuis, *Philosophy of Education*, p. 130.

[7]   For example, Broudy puts forth the concept of "the good life" as the ultimate purpose of education. By this he means the good life in this world. Harry S. Broudy, *Building a Philosophy of Education* (Prentice-Hall, 1954).

principles of life (souls) are created individually and immediately by God. God has stamped His image upon human persons by giving them intellects and wills: the power to understand, reason, and remember; and the power to make free decisions. The ultimate ground of human dignity is that we are created as persons in God's image, and consequently endowed by nature with intelligence and free will.[8]

Heredity and environment (environment includes education) can pressure people to believe and act in a certain way. Neither heredity nor environment however, negates the innate human potential for free choice. Further, the great variety of talents and abilities human persons have may trace its source not only indirectly to heredity and environment, but directly to the creativity of God.

Human persons are destined to live a life of friendship with God, beginning in the obscurity of faith in this life and finding fulfillment in the beatific vision in the next. This privileged friendship implies a life of unselfishness toward God and others, reflecting the total self-giving characteristic of the inner life of the Father, Son, and Holy Spirit. God's infinite joy comes from self-giving; human joy comes from the same source. Human persons can experience the joy of self-giving even in this life, a deep joy not even suffering can take away. It is in this sense that human purpose and fulfillment derive from friendship with God.

We intend to emphasize another dimension of human destiny in our school. Friendship with God is personal, but it is also communal and social. People are called to unselfishness not only as individuals, but also as partners in building the Kingdom of God. Every human achievement, made holy by grace, helps build this Kingdom, from the efforts of school children to master their studies, to the good work of fathers and mothers in Christian families. No acts inspired by grace and love will be consigned to obscurity. Not only will all good actions contribute to building the Kingdom in this life, but God will, moreover, lift

---

[8]   We found a helpful summary of Catholic teaching on human nature, as seen from an educator's perspective in Herbert Johnston, *A Philosophy of Education* (McGraw-Hill, 1963), pp. 29-46.

up all those good actions on the last day, and incorporate them into the new heaven and the new earth.[9] The expectation that every one of their unselfish actions here on earth will shine in heaven forever is the glorious vision we offer to children in our school.

Because they are creatures, human beings cannot achieve God's friendship on their own. Further, original sin has darkened the mind and weakened the will.[10] We need God's help: grace. Jesus Christ won grace for us. His sacrifice restored to us the potential for a supernatural life, a life above our nature: the potential Adam's sin had lost. Jesus continues to pour God's grace out on us through His Body, the Church, and particularly through the Mass and the other Sacraments. We fully recognize our dependence on God in every aspect of our school life. We try our best to avoid Pelagianism,[11] the heresy that claims we are capable of serving God by human effort alone.

How People Acquire Knowledge. God is the Principal Agent in the communication of knowledge, since God is the author of human intellectual power. The student is the

---

[9] "But we are taught that God is preparing a new dwelling place and a new earth...whose blessedness will answer and surpass all the longings for peace which spring up in the human heart.... While we are warned that it profits a man nothing if he gain the whole world and lose himself, the expectation of a new earth must not weaken but rather stimulate our concern for cultivating this one.... For after we have obeyed the Lord, and in His Spirit nurtured on earth the values of human dignity, brotherhood and freedom, and indeed all the good fruits of our nature and enterprise, we will find them again, but freed of stain, burnished and transfigured, when Christ hands over to the Father a kingdom eternal and universal; 'a kingdom of truth and life, of holiness and grace, of justice, love and peace.' On this earth that kingdom is already present in mystery. When the Lord returns, it will be brought into full flower." Vatican II, *Pastoral Constitution on the Church in the Modern World* (Vatican Archive Edition), n. 39.

[10] We found a good treatment of the effects of original sin on education in William J. McGucken, *The Catholic Way in Education* (Loyola, 1962), pp. 19-26. We also pondered Pius XI, *Christian Education*, n. 59.

[11] Pelagianism, a heresy of the fourth century, much opposed by St. Augustine, has plagued the Church through the years, and is alive and well in America today. According to Pelagianism, the purpose of divine grace is merely to facilitate what the human will can do by itself, and grace is always given in proportion to one's merits. Additional information: J. Ferguson, *Pelagius: A Historical and Theological Study* (Cambridge Press, 1956).

secondary efficient cause of his own knowledge. Under God, it is the *child* who learns.[12]

Knowledge begins with the senses[13]: contact with physical objects, such as mountains, tables, people and daisies, impresses images on the imagination. Words and other symbols containing ideas also enter through the senses. For example, a teacher may explain how clouds form, or the meaning of patriotism. The intellect may then choose to consider what the senses have presented, and subsequently the intellect may formulate ideas, providing understanding. In addition to understanding the immediately presented data, the mind may combine new ideas with ideas already present, may make logical inferences (deductions), or may make generalizations (inductions). Anywhere along the line the mind may *judge* whether to accept or reject an idea. Acceptance may arise from personal discovery, as when a student experiences that two oranges plus two oranges equal four oranges. Guided discovery may elicit acceptance, as when a teacher leads a student through the proof that the earth is round.[14] Authority may be a basis for acceptance, as when students believe that Dickens wrote *David Copperfield* because the teacher, who is trustworthy, tells them so. (Much of what human beings accept throughout their lives is based on belief in the word of others.) In the end, the mind may contain truth or error, depending on whether affirmations conform to reality or not. For that reason, Thomist philosophers today place much stress on the quality of the process enabling the mind to grasp as clearly as possible--if only in a limited way--what is actually present in reality.[15]

---

[12]   Anthony D. Gulley, *A Philosophical Study of the Efficient Causes of Learning According to St. Thomas Aquinas*, (Catholic University Press, 1961), pp. 13 ff.

[13]   As Thomists, we believe that there is nothing in the intellect which is not first in the senses. St. Thomas Aquinas, *De Veritate*, Q. 10, Art. 7, English translation by Robert W. Mulligan *et al.* (Hackett Publishing, 1994).

[14]   Aquinas, *Summa Theologica*, I, Q. 117, Art. 1.

[15]   Bernard Lonergan spent a lifetime showing how the Thomistic concept of knowing works out in the dynamics of practice. Not all would agree entirely with his position, including ourselves, but there is no doubt that he has greatly advanced the struggle to

Implications for Our School. Children learn many things on their own. But teachers may help speed up the learning process, extend its scope, and encourage children to become ever more skillful in mining knowledge from reality.

Teachers may offer raw experience (data)--contact with words, images, or other symbols that express ideas or facts; or contact with physical objects or activities. Teachers may help students to understand the raw data that students experience; to associate present understanding to what students already know; and to make inferences and generalizations.[16] Teachers may guide students in a responsible process of accepting ideas (judgment), always respecting students' freedom, just as God does. Teachers accomplish this process at times by encouraging personal discovery; at times by explaining the discovery process available in the human heritage; and at times by proposing an idea worthy of acceptance because God has revealed that idea, or the teacher, a trustworthy authority, has said that the idea is worthy of acceptance.

Finally, teachers may teach students how to remember facts, once students know and understand those facts. Progressives, by reacting with such hostility to uninspired rote memorization, have almost succeeded in eliminating "remembering" from the very concept of education.[17] Progressives apparently think that little effort needs to go into making sure children remember what they have learned. Memory is God's gift, so we believe that one of the aims of schooling should be to develop and enhance this gift. Wounded as we all are by original sin, children find not

---

understand the dynamics of the human mind, within the context of the Thomistic horizon of modified (critical) realism.   Bernard Lonergan, *Insight: A Study of Human Understanding* (Philosophical Library, 1957), Chapters IX, X, XIII.   We found a summary of his theory of knowledge in F. E. Crowe, ed., *Collection: Papers by Bernard Lonergan* (Herder and Herder, 1967), pp. 221-239 and 252-267. Lonergan gave a series of lectures on education at Xavier University in Cincinnati. We found the lectures stimulating, even though the treatment referred primarily to university education. *Collected Works*, vol. 10.

[16]   "Nothing should be required of the child without an explanation and without making sure that the child has understood." Maritain, *Crossroads*, p. 16.

[17]   Our conjecture is that failure to train the memory is one of the principal reasons for the public's dissatisfaction with schooling today.

only word-for-word memorization, but all memory work difficult. Our culture exposes everyone to so many rapid-fire images, providing instant gratification born of shallow experience, that memory can easily atrophy. Instead of giving in to this trend, we require our elementary students to learn by heart certain basics: for example, the multiplication table, vocal prayers, the ten commandments, some beautiful poems. Remembering other facts and ideas is also a requirement, but not necessarily word-for-word. Examples include the definition of a verb, the cases of pronouns, the capital of China, stories in the Bible, the meaning of the Mass.[18]

What children are capable of doing in elementary school depends on their level of development. "Whatever is received is received according to the measure of the recipient." At first the emphasis is on simple understanding and remembering raw experience. We do not expect first graders to do much logical deduction or inductive research. It is only in later grades that pupils will be able to understand the reasoning behind the conclusions taught, and to begin to do independent, critical thinking.[19]

On the other hand, we do not intend to place a cap on children's ability to learn by failing to challenge each child. We do not wish to underestimate students' capacity. Neither do we intend to shield pupils, in the name of self-esteem, from the consequences of failure to put forth the necessary effort. Self-esteem, built on genuine achievement, must be based on hard work. We do not offer fake praise. Flattery does children more harm than good.[20]

---

[18]   In working with memory, we employ all four methods of remembering, as listed by St. Thomas, following Aristotle: association with an image (I remember my pain the day I fell out of the tree); orderly sequence of matter (I organize my ideas so they will be easier to remember); engagement to remember (I remember the team strategy, because I want to win the game); distributed practice (I impress it on my memory by the repetition involved in drill). Aquinas, *Summa Theologica*, II-II, Q.49, Art. 1.

[19]   Giussani believes that children are ready to begin critical thinking at about age ten. Luigi Giussani, *The Risk of Education* (Crossroads, 2001), p. 9.

[20]   Maureen Stout develops this point at length in *Feel-Good Curriculum*, pp. 127-132

We are ready to accept any method of teaching, old or new, that serves our purpose.[21]   Before introducing methods into our school, however, we want to evaluate those methods. We want to be confident that teaching methods do not obscure or deny what we believe about the nature of truth, moral goodness, human destiny, grace, and the learning process.

If false assumptions about any of these topics remain embedded in the methods we use, we risk teaching children implicitly something other than what we want them to know.

Presuming that the assumptions underlying specific teaching methods are acceptable, a combination of considerations will enter into a teacher's choice to employ a given classroom method. These considerations include: how well the method promotes understanding and remembering, the developmental capacity of the student, the nature of the subject matter, the teacher's own skills, and the time available for teaching what we want our children to learn. The importance of time is not to be underestimated. We expect our students to learn a specified number of things during their nine years with us. We do not look favorably on methods so cumbersome or time-consuming that this full measure of learning is unlikely to occur.

What the School Is Supposed to Do. Dewey asked himself, "What kind of schools do we need in order to make democracy work?"   In his response, Dewey described the school as a microcosm of the larger society, where learning is connected to the child's own world of experience. Such schools, in Dewey's view, are privileged places where young citizens realize growth in their store of experience and learn to work together in solving practical problems. Thus the larger society becomes worthy, lovely, and harmonious.

Our question was, "What kind of school do we need to help our children become good citizens both of this world and the next?" We see our school not so much a microcosm of the larger society, or even of the Church, but as a limited setting,

[21]   Ravitch, *Left Behind*, p. 453.

encompassing only part of children's lives, namely the six or seven hours in the school day. While studying and learning in school, however, our students live within a social system based on the ideals of Jesus, directed by people who believe in Him, a social system that expects children to act according to Christ's teaching. Both the "teaching" and the "setting" make our school what we want it to be.

Our position on truth, morality, human nature and destiny, learning, and the purpose of schools forms the obvious basis for our school to be different.[22] What we have said so far will serve as background for the next chapter about our school's nature, context, purpose and goals.

Progressive education theory, although flawed at the core by an erroneous concept of truth, and by absence of belief in original sin, grace, and eternity, contains some elements we may accept and take to heart. These are: paying greater attention to the child being taught, taking a more humane approach to teaching, and bringing schooling closer to life.[23] By way of illustration, a member of our Core Group told what it was like to attend a progressive school many years ago:

> Our teacher was the kindly Miss Wagner, and I
> learned many things in her second grade class. I
> developed an interest in reading (all to the
> good). Through a field trip to a dairy farm, I
> learned that milk did not come from grocery
> stores. From knitting a potholder, I learned a
> multitude of ways in which the inattentive
> learner may make mistakes. From building a

---

[22]   "It would be a mistake to think that the education of Christians by Christians is necessarily a Christian education. It is not so unless all the elements that enter into the complete formation of youth are deliberately conceived and purposefully employed in view of producing a definitely Christian temper of mind, and will, and judgment." Edward Leen, *What is Education?* (Sheed & Ward, 1944), p. 6. Many authorities have discussed how a Catholic school is to be different. We found a helpful summary of the thought of Spalding, Doupanloup, Newman, and Mercier in Franz DeHovre, *Catholicism in Education* (Benziger, 1934), pp. 165-382.

[23]   Maritain agrees. *Crossroads*, pp. 16, 118.

birdhouse, I gained a new appreciation of the domestic habits of birds. By planting grass seed in an orange crate, I experienced the thrill of watching new life. I learned to take a less dim view of vegetables, by being assigned to play a turnip in the school play. My education did not suffer overmuch, however, by my exposure to child-centered education. Next year I was back in Catholic school, where Sr. Mary St. Peter very quickly brought me up to snuff.[24]

---

[24] Our Core Group affirmed broadening of the child's experience as a valuable element in human development, but believes that most of the activities described here would be more fittingly incorporated into leisure-time activities such as Scouting or YMCA/YWCA, rather than school.

4.

What We Want Our School to Be

Nature, Purpose, and Goals

O U R S C H O O L, *established to assist parents in the education of their children, is part of the ministry of our parish.* The school takes its place alongside the other dimensions of our parish ministry--nurture of the faithful, ecumenism, evangelization of the unchurched, charity and justice, and support for the diocese and universal Church. We subsidize our school, and operate it under the direction of our bishop and his representatives.[1] Our school is the apple of our eye.

Our school assists parents in the education of their children. Parents do not control the school, but parents' insights are always welcome. Parents who choose to send their children here, however, may reasonably expect certain specified types of help in fulfilling their God-given responsibilities toward their children.

We are fully aware that ours is not the only type of Catholic school.[2] Our school serves children who are practicing

---

[1] The bishop decides what is to be taught in parochial schools, basing his judgment on the needs of children in the diocese. Canons 803, 806.

Catholics, most of whom are members of our own parish. We are not an ecumenical school, although we do admit a limited number of non-Catholic children, provided they are faithful to the practice of their own religion.

We have chosen to define our school as serving practicing Catholics, believing that the best way of serving our non-practicing children is to give them and their families personalized spiritual direction in our Ananias Home Tutoring Program. Children in this program, who have advanced enough in their relationship to Jesus to begin to participate in the Mass,[3] may then be enrolled in our school. In this way we show special love for our non-practicing children, at the same time insuring that we do not unwittingly trivialize religion, by acting as though participation in a Catholic school somehow defines a faithful Catholic, even apart from attendance at Mass. In the past, this false assumption was widespread in our locality; consequently, very few of our students were assisting at Mass.

Background and Context. Established in 1924, our school consists of kindergarten through eighth grade, and enrolls about two hundred students. In addition to the principal and classroom teachers, we have part-time instructors in music, art, physical education, and wraparound religion. There is also a librarian/computer teacher and a kindergarten aide. Outside agencies provide tutoring, nursing services, psychological testing, and counseling. All school personnel are laity.

Parishioners represent eighty percent of our students; Catholics from other parishes, eight percent; and non-Catholics, twelve percent. Most families are of German descent. Students of other racial/ethnic backgrounds are very few, approximating the mix in the local population. Most parents show a great

[2]   Other types include: schools for everyone, schools with no Catholic students, hedge schools in times of persecution, literacy schools in primitive areas, schools that serve both practicing and non-practicing Catholics, schools in impoverished areas, ecumenical schools with Catholic participation, regional schools, religious order schools, boarding schools, schools for migrant workers or immigrants. The list could be expanded. Our supposition is that each type would have important variations in goals and programs.

[3]   For nuances and additional details, see pp. 86 ff.

interest in their children, who are well cared-for at home and supported in a variety of elective activities.

Not all of our families provide a home environment conducive to high academic achievement. Some parents, modest in their educational expectations, place a higher value on non-school areas of their children's life. Not many graduates of our school plan to attend a four-year college, preferring to enter the skilled work force through apprenticeships or similar programs.

A special linguistic challenge for our school is the existence of faulty speech patterns in this area--double negatives, errors in verb forms and errors in the use of pronouns.

Our children take the *Iowa Tests of Cognitive Ability and Scholastic Achievement*, mandated by the diocese. The scholastic achievement of most students somewhat exceeds their cognitive ability. As a school, we fall into the average range of achievement, compared to the nation as a whole.

Although old, our school building is well maintained, and has a cheerful and neat appearance. The chief disadvantages are the pedestrian architecture, the small windows, and one undersized classroom. Air-conditioning provides comfort during the hot days of fall and spring. The parish gym, a large building, houses the school library and lunchroom, and provides space for assemblies and physical education. The playground is adequate, and is bordered by large trees. In one corner of a grassy area, also used as a playground, there is a small building on which our art students have painted replicas of trees found in the Easter garden of Fra Angelico. As in most Catholic schools, students wear uniforms.

Thirty-eight percent of the parish's ordinary income goes to support the school. Tuition is modest, and financial supplements are available, with minimal red tape, especially to families with more than one child in the school. No parishioner is refused entrance into our school for inability to pay the tuition. Non-Catholic students are charged higher tuition than Catholics, under the assumption that Protestant churches might be interested in helping their students financially, just as Catholic congregations do for theirs. Our parish operates a Thrift Shop, which provides some $40,000 per year in tuition assistance and other aid. Because we are a tithing parish with no debt, we have little difficulty keeping the tuition low, and participating in the diocesan program for enhancing teachers' salaries.

Established in 1904, our parish now contains 923 families and 2,350 parishioners. Families are mostly skilled working class, with a few professionals. There is one priest. Volunteerism is high, and Sunday Mass attendance is fifty percent. Located in an older, well-kept section of the city, the parish territory offers little prospect for population expansion. Housing falls into three groups: modest houses with medium-size yards, where flowers and children abound; row houses, containing older people, or couples just getting started; and more elaborate homes on substantial lots.

Parish mobility is fairly high, with an average of seventy families joining and seventy leaving each year for the past eight years. The economy, based principally on a large number of diversified manufacturing establishments, is stable. Unemployment is low, and people move here to obtain jobs. The work ethic is quite strong. The age structure of the parish and of the community follows the national pattern. Historically, the religious climate has been heavily influenced by the Lutheran and Reformed Churches. At present, both Catholics and conservative evangelicals are rapidly increasing in number. The community's ethnic composition is German, although other groups, especially Hispanics, are beginning to move in. There are very few African Americans.

Not only parents, but grandparents, relatives and many other parishioners take a great interest in the children and their activities. Thirty-four percent of school-age parishioners attend the school. Members of the parish give voluntary service and provide financial support. Affection for the school is underscored by the fact that many parents and grandparents of current students are graduates themselves.

Purpose. The ultimate purpose of our school is to give glory to God, for what He is in Himself, and for what He has done for us. Within God's inner life, the Father, Son and Holy Spirit relate to one another with infinite unselfishness; in this total self-giving God's happiness consists. God has freely chosen to share His happiness with us. Our school gives glory to God by helping parents prepare their children to participate in God's unselfishness and happiness in this life, looking forward to ultimate participation in the next.[4]

Created in God's image, endowed with particular clusters of talents,[5] and destined for eternal life, children have great dignity, possessing a freedom that God honors and respects. Through original sin, however, minds have been darkened and wills have been weakened. In order to fulfill their destiny, children need the grace that comes from Christ through the Church.

Destined to a created share in God's inner life, the children's present vocation is to prepare themselves, through activities inside and outside the school, to grow in a personal relationship with God, and participate as members of society in building the Kingdom.[6] We make sure our pupils know that it is human achievement, both personal and social, made holy by grace, that God will lift up on the last day, and incorporate into the new heaven and the new earth.

Children, weakened by original sin, often find study burdensome. Sometimes they find it hard to be good and are in need of repentance.[7] The grace we all need comes from Christ through the Church. After the Fall caused by original sin, God sent His Son to re-open heaven, show us by word and example how to live, and give us the help (grace) to live according to His will.

Like all Catholic schools, our school is grounded in the inner life of the Blessed Trinity. Jesus draws us to this life

---

[4] Kevin J. O'Brien, *The Proximate Aim of Education* (Catholic University of America, 1958), pp. 73-174.

[5] Aquinas, *Summa Theologica*, I, Q.96, Art.3; I, Q.85, Art 7.

[6] Speaking of young people in Toronto on July 31, 2002, John Paul II said, "They must learn to build, brick by brick, the city of God within the city of man."

[7] In describing the effects of the fall, Genesis speaks of the earth as bringing forth "thorns and thistles" (Gen 3:17). In cultivating the mind, the human person often encounters thorns and thistles. Learning is not always fun.

through the Church, her teaching, Sacraments and guidance. One of Jesus' principal ways of bringing us to a created share in the Trinity's life is through the Mass. In the Mass, Jesus gathers up the sacrifices of the assembled community, joining the peoples' sacrifices to His one great act of love on the cross. That is why we view our school, as we view all of life, as an extension and living-out of the Mass.

Goals. We have two goals: one direct, the other indirect. The direct goal of our school is to see to it that children acquire the knowledge that they need. The indirect goal is to provide a setting that will encourage children to progress in the Christian life. We believe that both goals are important for achieving our general purpose of helping parents educate their children as Christian citizens of this life and the next. But we believe that everyone must understand clearly the distinction between the two goals, so that in carrying out the one we will not inadvertently neglect the other.

We call the one goal *direct*, because the means used to achieve knowledge can be directly tied to a verifiable result, as an effect to a cause. We call the other goal *indirect*, because providing a Christian setting will not guarantee children's advancement in the Christian life, even though we hope it will be a strong influence.[8]

Our direct and indirect goals, although distinct in nature, are complementary, and contribute, each in its own way, to the school's ultimate purpose. We enlighten our students by knowledge. We provide a school setting where children can receive good example, where all are expected to act in a Christian manner, and where each child can develop habits of virtue. We do all these things so that children may advance in holiness, for the greater glory of God.

---

[8] Adapted from an insight of Maritain. *Crossroads,* pp. 25-28.

Indirect Goal. Our indirect goal is to provide a setting for schooling[9] that will encourage children to draw closer to the Lord.

Children attend our school six and one-half hours a day, five days a week, nine months a year. The better the school lives up to its ideals, the greater opportunity the school provides for children to experience how Christianity works in practice. Within the school, children receive inspiration and support. But through the good example of their own Christian life, they are able to contribute as well as benefit, to give as well as receive.

Our school is limited in scope. We do not think of the parish school as *the* most important setting for Christian experience. The family and the parish are that.[10] The reason for our enthusiasm for Catholic schools, however, is their significant role through the centuries in helping parents raise their children, and the potential for schools to play an even more significant role today. In our day the general culture offers little support for the Christian life. Parents need all the help they can get.

When we tried to define for ourselves what we mean by a Christian setting, we listed eight elements:

1. We try to have good *teachers*, who will mirror the love of God in their own hearts, and love the children in their care. That mirroring of God's love means taking an interest in each child, treating children with respect, encouraging initiative within reasonable and stable boundaries, and

---

[9]   We use the word "setting" rather than "community", because our school does not include enough aspects of life to qualify as a community in the technical sense. We do try, however, to have the same sense of unity within our school as that of a true community. In his compelling apologetic for Catholic schools, O'Neill contends that schools today are much more intensive and influential social systems than they were years ago. Michael O'Neill, *New Schools in a New Church* (St. John's University, Collegeville, 1971), p. 34.

[10]   It is Maritain's opinion that moral education is more the task of the family and the parish than the school. The school is more concerned with intelligence and knowledge. Jacques Maritain, "Typical Aspects of Christian Education", in Edmund Fuller, ed., *The Christian Idea of Education* (Yale University Press, 1957), p. 188.

challenging children to study hard even when studying is not fun. Since our school exists to assist parents, we expect teachers to work in full collaboration with the parents who entrust their children to our school.

2. We offer children *Christian motivation* for what children do in school. Ultimate motivation is to give glory to God. They glorify God by living out their present vocation to develop their talents as citizens of this world and the next.

3. We encourage a spirit of *joy* in learning and in school life. We teach that joy is not incompatible with the cross. We also make ample provision for children to practice the virtue of *eutrapelia*,[11] by engaging in spirited recreation that refreshes them and helps them do their best.

4. We make provision for *repentance*, for those who have given offense.

5. We offer children a number of *religious experiences*: retreats, weekly Mass, the Sacrament of Penance, Forty Hours, May Devotions, Stations of the Cross, Holy Week activities, First Communion and Confirmation celebrations, prayer groups; guidance in volunteering in school, parish and community; options for leadership in initiating and organizing good works; and several occasions for children to choose to make religion a priority in their lives.

6. We insist on *courtesy* in the relationships among students, teachers and parents.

7. We provide a *pleasant physical environment,* including good art in hallways—some classical, some contemporary, and some religious.

8. We try to operate our school in such a way that we *trust in God* rather than in our own efforts. Such trust undergirds school policies. For example, prayer pervades the school day, especially prayer for success in learning. We aim to do as well as possible what God calls us to do, putting aside worldly competition with other school systems and

---

[11] Aquinas, *Summa Theologica*, II-II, Q.168, Art 2.

the temptation to overextend ourselves. We make sure that the cloud of mortal sin does not hang heavy over our school, by requiring Catholic children to be faithful to attendance at Mass.

Direct Goal. We teach children to "*understand*" and "*remember*", and we make sure, through testing, that understanding and remembering have actually occurred.[12] Although we teach children with authority, we respect their human freedom, and are ready to persuade rather than pressure them to "*judge*" that our teaching is true.[13] Consequently we try to help children, according to each one's capacity, to understand the reasonableness of what we teach, to integrate more advanced knowledge with the knowledge they already have, and to align all learning with the Catholic vision of human destiny in this life and the next.

We are an elementary school.[14] As such, our highest priority is to teach those basic language, computational and religious facts, ideas and skills that the dignity of every Christian civilized person requires. Beyond that, we follow the curriculum our diocese prescribes.[15] We make use of services provided by the government, but our ability to teach exceptionally slow or exceptionally talented children is otherwise limited. Within the scope of freedom permitted by our diocese, we are careful not to duplicate educational opportunities more fittingly provided by parents or readily available in parish or community. We are not in competition with the public school or other community

---

[12] Simple exposure to experience may have a part to play in human development, but we see our school primarily as an agent of understanding and remembering. Thus we see little value in elementary school classwork which merely "covers matter," without time or effort devoted to insuring that what has been taught has actually been learned.

[13] Byrnes, *John Paul II and Educating for Life,* p. 127.

[14] As we reviewed the educational literature, it was often difficult to tell what level of education the author was discussing. We were always asking ourselves, "Is the author speaking of a first grader or a graduate student?" [Dear Scholars, Please take this as a very mild complaint.]

[15] We describe our approach to curriculum as "basics plus".

agencies. We focus our attention on what we believe children *absolutely need to learn while they are in elementary school.* In our view, that is no insignificant contribution.

During their years in our school, students of necessity develop a certain degree of skill in learning. Since we are an elementary school, however, we have chosen to place our emphasis on *what*[16] is learned, rather than on *learning how to learn,* on knowledge rather than on process. We understand that in high school and college, the emphasis will gradually shift to *learning how to learn.*[17]

Truth is one, whether truth comes into the mind through reason, revelation, or a combination of both. A goal of Catholic education has traditionally been to help the student understand the unity of truth, and the relationship of the various branches of knowledge to one another, culminating in philosophy and theology. This idea is not new. Origen established the very first formal Catholic school at Alexandria in the year 212. That school exhibited the

> ...excitement inherent in the mind's search for
> intellectual order, for the hierarchy in the order
> of truth, for the inner hidden unity that must
> somehow join in a many-splendored,
> differentiated pattern all the fragments of truth,
> human and divine, that the intelligence of man
> can encompass.... This love of the ordered
> wisdom of the Gospel, guiding intelligence—
> itself greatly loved—in all its free ranging, was
> for Gregory of Neocaesarea [Origen's pupil] the
> glowing heart of his school experience. It

---

[16] Shields thought the emphasis in Catholic schools should shift from content to process, but we disagree. Thomas E. Shields, *Philosophy of Education* (Catholic Educational Press, 1917), p. 243.

[17] W. Kane, *Some Principles of Education* (Loyola, 1938), p. 172.

> remains forever the heart of the school
> experience, when the school is Christian.[18]

Although this Christian integration of knowledge is a clear educational aim, the difficulty of achieving such an aim is evident in a world inundated with information. Further, this goal would seem to be more suited to higher education than to elementary school. We mention Christian integration here to make clear that we do affirm this goal, as part of a comprehensive Catholic view of education.[19]

We make no apology for making the acquisition of knowledge the direct goal of our school. As Thomists, we believe in the central importance of cultivating the mind, because possession of truth perfects the faculty which first of all serves to make us human.[20] We are also conscious of the role that knowledge plays, along with grace, in moving the will to accept what is good and do what is right.[21]

This, then, is what our school is, and what we want it to be:

1. It is a parish ministry.

---

[18] John Courtney Murray, in Fuller, *Christian Idea of Education,* pp. 158-159. Others who have treated this theme: Benedict Ashley, "Introduction", in McInerny, *Common Things,* p. 12; Ellis A. Joseph, in Hunt, *Research on Catholic Education,* pp. 52-53; Buetow, *Catholic School,* p. 109; Vincent E. Smith, *The School Experience* (Bruce, 1960); NCCB, *To Teach as Jesus Did,* n. 103; Pius XI, *Christian Education,* n. 80.

[19] In our *Wraparound Religion* program we tried a modest experiment with our eighth grade. We tried to get students to understand that all the things they were learning in religion class fit together into a whole, and were not just isolated bits of knowledge. We presented the Blessed Trinity as the ultimate reality; Jesus and His Body, the Church, as our way to the Trinity; and our response as a personal relationship to the Trinity within the communion of the Church. We did not have much success with our experiment, but we intend to keep on trying.

[20] Aquinas, *Summa Theologica,* I-II, Q. 94, Art. 2.

[21] Here we have chosen to follow Maritain's opinion regarding the direct and indirect goals of a Catholic school. Maritain, *Crossroads,* pp. 25-28. Cunningham agrees: *Pivotal Problems,* pp. 556 ff.

2. It helps parents fulfill their responsibility for bringing up their children.

3. It enrolls children who are practicing their religion (a few of whom are Protestants). Evangelization of the unchurched is not its focus.

4. Its ultimate purpose is to give glory to God.

5. It views the children it serves in light of Catholic teaching on the human person: created in God's image with particular talents, weakened by original sin, redeemed by Christ, needing grace that comes through the Church, destined to eternal life.

6. The direct goal of our school is knowledge. As an elementary school, its highest priority is to teach children to *understand* and *remember* those basic language, computational and religious facts, ideas and skills that the dignity of every Christian civilized person requires. As time allows, we teach beyond the basics.

7. The indirect goal of our school is to provide a *setting for learning* that will encourage children to draw closer to the Lord. We create this setting by loving the children in our care; offering each child Christian motivation; encouraging a spirit of joy; making provision for repentance; offering a number of religious experiences; providing occasions for making religion a priority; insisting on courtesy among students, teachers and parents; providing a pleasant physical environment; and basing our policies and procedures on trust in God.

The story of what happened when we tried to infuse this understanding of nature, purpose, and goals into the lifeblood of our school will be told in the chapters that follow.

5.

Teachers Make the School

"As the heart makes the home, the teacher makes the school. What we need above all things, wherever the young are gathered for education, is not a showy building, or costly apparatus, or improved methods or text-books, but a living, loving, illuminated human being who has deep faith in the power of education and a real desire to bring it to bear upon those who are entrusted to him."[1]

When St. John Baptist de LaSalle began his work of establishing Catholic elementary schools in seventeenth-century France, his first concern was teachers.[2] LaSalle knew that if the teachers were what he wanted them to be, the school would be what he wanted it to be also.

Likewise it seemed obvious to our Core Group that teachers should be our first concern. Teachers' actions will be an

---

[1] John Lancaster Spalding, *Means and Ends of Education* (McClurg, 1909), p. 133.

[2] The story is told in Edward A. Fitzpatrick, *LaSalle: Patron of All Teachers* (Bruce, 1951), pp. 138-148, 272-295. De LaSalle's ideas became the basis for teacher formation in the great teaching orders that arose in France in the nineteenth century, and had a great influence on the development of the modern Catholic school. We found an illustration of this influence in Sarah A. Curtis, *Educating the Faithful: Religion, Schooling, and Society in Nineteenth-Century France* (Northern Illinois University Press, 2000).

expression of what is deep inside of them; they will find a way to influence the children in their care. Teachers will teach in such a way that their very imparting of knowledge will inspire their students to love the Lord.[3]

Spiritual and Professional Support.   Before beginning to teach here, our teachers need a course on Catholic elementary education.   Such a course should familiarize teachers with the Catholic philosophical-theological position on the nature of truth, the nature of human persons and human destiny, how people acquire knowledge, the purpose and goals of various types of Catholic elementary schools, and Catholic critiques of popular educational methods and motivational systems. Teachers need an overview of the history and key figures in our educational tradition.   A further need is an introduction to the concepts that form the cultural world of the children our teachers will teach.   We have in mind an educational experience that will awaken interest, inspire, and open doors to future study.

Preparatory studies, however, are not enough.   How will our teachers *continue* to benefit from support in their professional and spiritual lives?[4]   When we had nuns teaching in our school, their religious congregations provided this support.   Today our teachers are lay persons.   These loyal and good lay persons have degrees and are faithful in their religious duties.   Most of these teachers, however, have family responsibilities that limit leisure traditionally available to members of religious communities for spiritual and professional development.

In light of these circumstances, we decided that time for spiritual and professional development must be a key feature in the regime of the school year: normal operating procedure. Spiritual and professional development takes time.   If we cannot

[3]   We were inspired by Thomas Groome's approach to spirituality for teachers.   Thomas H. Groome, *Educating for Life: A Spiritual Vision for Every Teacher and Parent* (Thomas More, 1998), Chapter 7.

[4]   We found a strong statement of principles on lay formation in *Lay Catholics in Schools: Witnesses to Faith* (Sacred Congregation for Catholic Education, 1982), nn. 60-70.

afford to pay teachers for this needed time, we cannot afford a Catholic school.

Of course, our teachers do receive continuing support for their spiritual lives within their parish communities. And in our school teachers gather daily for prayer before the Blessed Sacrament. But if in the past nuns needed an annual retreat of several days, certainly today's lay teachers, to be "*in* the world but not *of* the world", need no less.

Local colleges and dioceses provide courses in subject matter, psychology, and teaching methods, and teachers regularly take advantage of these opportunities. But teachers need an annual seminar of several days' duration in order to delve more deeply into the foundational principles of Catholic education.

To be practical, retreats and seminars will have to be scheduled so that lay teachers can be home with their families by evening.

Financial Support. From a secular perspective, our teachers are employees subject to civil taxes and the like; but from a religious perspective they are Ministers of Catholic Schooling. Our teachers are semi-volunteers, since, according to diocesan policy, they receive compensation that is only seventy-five percent of what local public school teachers receive. We recruit our Ministers of Schooling precisely as semi-volunteers; their willingness to serve as such constitutes part of the school's endowment. We list the dollar amount of their contributed services on the parish financial report, and make clear to parents and parishioners that teachers are supporting the school financially in this way.

Teachers are sometimes at that point in their lives where family obligations do not permit them to continue as semi-volunteers on the compensation we offer. We make it clear to teachers when they come to us that under such circumstances they may have to leave our school, at least for a while, until family obligations once again permit them to minister on a semi-volunteer basis.

In fairness to our children, we expect teachers to honor the contract they sign in April to teach in our school the following year. It has sometimes happened in the past that public school districts have offered lucrative teaching positions to one or another of our teachers late in August. However, since we stated in a formal letter that teachers were not to circulate their resumes after they had signed with us, no such circumstance has intervened to leave our school without a teacher. In our letter we said that except in extreme emergencies, no teacher was to come to us with a request to be released from our contract. If teachers *must* make such a request, we will of course release them, but we will not like it. From the time we made our thinking clear, there have been no inappropriate requests. With rare exceptions, our teachers remain with us year after year. They like teaching here, and we like them.

Teachers and Parents. The role of teachers is to help parents in the education of their children. Teachers and parents need not always be in full agreement. But teachers and parents do need to be in frequent communication—formally and informally. Our hope is for a deeply spiritual rapport between teachers and parents, always grounded in the good of the child.

Parents help the school in many ways--through volunteer service and through continuing moral support. The Home and School Association, in its reconstituted form, promotes spirituality, arranges talks on topics of parental interest, and cooperates with teachers and staff in providing invaluable classroom and clerical assistance. There is only a small amount of fund-raising each year.[5] The association does not discuss school policy.

Parents, with the encouragement of teachers and staff, do offer invaluable insights and wisdom on matters of policy and practice, formally through the *Spring Survey,* and informally whenever parents have something to suggest throughout the year. Parents with the inclination and time to read philosophical

---

[5] Fund-raising projects require the principal's approval, which is given in conjunction with the review of the association's annual budget.

and technical books and work assiduously on educational issues, may nominate themselves for appointment to the School Committee of the Parish Advisory Council, a group with great influence in the school. The School Committee is always seeking working members.

Parents of new students receive a four-hour orientation and sign a *Memorandum of Agreement*[6] before we permit them to register their children in our school. Returning students' parents signify their support for school policies by signing an annual *Affirmation Statement.* Most of these parents studied our *Handbook* carefully before signing. On first encounter, the new approaches surprised and sometimes chagrined those few who did not study the *Handbook.* We note, however, that as the years pass, we have come closer to one of the principal goals of the renewal project: the unification of parental expectations.

---

[6] See page 89.

6.

Can Children Study for the Glory of God?

THE ULTIMATE PURPOSE of our school is to give glory to God. Can we translate this purpose into the motivation we offer to our students? Can we encourage our students to study and to live their school life as a way of showing their unselfish love of God? Can we create enthusiasm about building His Kingdom?

When we considered these questions, our Core Group decided to make creating this kind of enthusiasm a major objective. As our discussion progressed, we came to believe that Christian motivation should become the very hallmark of our school. As such, Christian motivation would be one of the elements that most sharply distinguished us from the public schools. In the literature on motivation in public schools, we found no hint that a higher purpose, or a purpose that did not end with this life, could motivate children.[1]

---

[1] We looked at a few works: Eva Dreikurs Ferguson, *Motivation: A Biosocial and Cognitive Integration of Motivation and Emotion* (Oxford University Press, 2000); Postman, *End of Education*; Alfie Kohn, *Punished by Rewards* (Houghton Mifflin, 1993); James P. Raffini, *One Hundred Fifty Ways to Increase Intrinsic Motivation in the Classroom* (Allyn and Bacon, 1996).

We took six approaches.

Prayer. We realized that from a purely human perspective, children raised in today's culture would be unlikely to respond positively to spiritual motivation for study. Who are we, however, to presume that with the help of grace, children would not respond? They are God's children. Inspiring them with Christian motivation would be a formidable and ongoing task. But God is all-powerful and grace is everywhere. We decided to rely on prayer. We put into the school prayer: "Receive all our good deeds, join them to Your sacrifice at the Mass, to the glory of God and the good of all the world." We moved ahead in trust and were not disappointed.

Example. Adults who truly love God and the children in their charge, and who are obviously happy, are a powerful example for imitation. That example is the reason why we have placed such emphasis on giving our teachers the opportunity for intensifying their personal relationship with God. And that example is the reason why we hope to hear our teachers telling, again and again in our classrooms, the stories of Jesus, the saints, and the martyrs.

Explanation. We encouraged our teachers to talk about God's goodness, and not just in religion class. Jesus came to earth to show us God's affection and to draw us into the unselfish life of the Father, Son, and Holy Spirit. He also taught us that our happiness consists in unselfishness that imitates the self-giving of the Three Divine Persons. The more generous and enthusiastic we are, the happier we will be, even in this life, in spite of the crosses that may come our way. It is our great privilege as human beings to employ our talents to help build the Kingdom, so God can use all our good deeds to create the new heaven and the new earth at the end of time. Every good deed children do in school, from the hard work of study, to the effort to avoid cliques, will become part of the new heavens and will live forever! The artisans who built Chartres were not just earning a living, but building a cathedral. Our students are not just learning things; they are building the Kingdom of God by the way they study and by the way they act. This is the vision we offer the children in our school.

We asked our teachers to make explicit connections between the vision and specific activities. Here are some examples.

When the cadets at Annapolis learn how to handle small sailboats, they are learning the fundamentals of navigation. Modern sea vessels are basically the same. If you can handle a sailboat now, you can learn to operate an aircraft carrier later. If you can handle the multiplication table now, you can learn quantum physics later. Basics are the foundation of advanced knowledge. The better the foundation, the stronger the building. The more you know, the more you can contribute to building the Kingdom of God. From this point of view, learning the multiplication table is very much a religious act.[2]

When you are kind to the members of your class who are not your special friends, you are showing respect for Christ who said, "As long as you did it to the least of my brethren, you did it to me" (Mt 25:45). Seeing Christ in all people is a basic virtue that builds the Kingdom, and you can learn to do it, with God's help, right here on the playground.

Interest. All knowledge is objectively interesting, because everything relating to God's truth is interesting. Teachers will try to evoke the interest already inherent in subject matter, so that children can taste the fullness of wonder in their learning experiences. In this respect, teachers follow the example of Jesus the Teacher, who spoke of the familiar in order to lead His hearers into the unfamiliar.[3] Christ used figures from daily life--

---

[2] We were happy to learn that the Diocese of Kansas City-St. Joseph made an explicit connection between religion and mathematics in its curriculum, employing the concepts of the dignity of the human person, the call to a specific history, and the call to life in community. Quoted in Merylann J. Schuttloffel, "Promises and Possibilities", in James Youniss, John Convey and Jeffrey McClellan, eds., *The Catholic Character of Catholic Schools* (Notre Dame, 2000), p. 119.

fields, dishes, houses, dinners, journeys. He told stories—"A certain man went down to Jericho..."(Lk 10:30). He asked questions—"Which of the two was neighbor?"...(Lk 10:36).

Not all of Jesus' listeners were interested in what He had to say. What could be of more interest than the Bread of Life? Yet some were not at all interested and walked away. We recognize that children will not always be interested in what they are being taught, even if the teacher is as skilled as Jesus in drawing the interest out. Some will walk away; original sin has darkened the human intellect. But children need not walk away. Children committed to God's glory will devote themselves to what they need to learn, even when the subjective notion that what they are studying is inherently interesting is slow to emerge, or even altogether absent.

Further, schoolchildren will often encounter the thorns and thistles springing up everywhere outside the Garden of Eden. The learning process, not always easy and pleasant, requires personal effort. Cardinal Newman said, "Knowledge often makes a bloody entrance into the head."

Our task is to give children loving encouragement to do in school what gives glory to God, even when such action involves the cross. Everything about school life, including the cross, may be offered to Jesus in the Mass; He delights to join each child's sacrifices with His as He glorifies the Father.

We provide the motivation and evoke the interest. But we *require* the child to work hard. In the end we test understanding and recall; if these are lacking we keep working until the child achieves success. No child passes along from grade to grade for purely social reasons.

Pushing the Limits. The idea of offering opportunity for students to push themselves to the limit scholastically came from watching them practice and play basketball. Children spend long hours, at great inconvenience, honing their athletic skills. In basketball drills players run up and down the gym floor countless

---

[3]   Teachers lead students from the familiar to the unfamiliar. Aquinas, *Summa Theologica*, I, Q.117, Art.1.

times without complaint. Team members must memorize complex diagrams of strategies and plays. After practice, weary but happy, the team returns home, energized by the prospect of giving their all in the upcoming game.

We asked ourselves, "Where is the motivation in all this?" The ultimate motivation is the glory of God. But the proximate motivation is the thrill of pushing themselves to the limit. These children seldom win the championship. At the end of the year their parents give a simple banquet, where all the players receive small trophies. The recognition is hardly in proportion to the effort the children have expended. We discovered the motivational key in the speeches at the banquet. Over and over the coaches, teachers and parents commended the hard work and the effort to play well. The children, thrilled to be able to push themselves to the limit, used to the full a talent God had given them for His glory.

From what we had observed, we decided to provide at least some opportunities for children to face other challenges squarely and experience the same thrill. We reasoned that if our parish could have a basketball tournament, we could have a grammar tournament. Poor grammar is endemic to our area, so we invited the Chamber of Commerce to sponsor the tournament. The business community was only too happy to do so, because local business has a decided interest in hiring graduates who can write grammatical sentences and know how to spell. A member of our Core Group devised the rules of the contest. The plan was to hold the tournament within our own school, and later to invite other schools to compete. In the end there will be recognition and publicity. But we expect the opportunity for children to push themselves to the limit for the glory of God will be the driving force.

Eliminating Bribes. We discovered that our teachers, under the influence of the behaviorism so widely prevalent in schools of teacher training, were bribing students to learn. Bribes took the form of candy, stars, pencils and other small reinforcements or rewards.[4] By demonstrating that you can get starved rats to push levers if you reward them with Rice Krispies, the behaviorist B. F. Skinner developed a theory of motivation for getting children to do what you want them to do. We found the behaviorist approach manipulative, and we very much objected to any analogy that compared children, who possess intelligence and free will, to rats. We asked our teachers to end the practice and to make use of the motivational system we have already explained.   The teachers complied with their customary graciousness. In addition, our pastor explained the new policy to the whole parish, in a homily entitled, "Our Children Are Not Rats".

Several years ago, the proposal for a voluntary reading program included dress-down days as a reinforcement. Rejecting this behavioristic inducement, our teachers elicited a spirit of enthusiasm for "Reading for the Kingdom".   The program has continued successfully to this day.

As a postscript, we must state that we are not opposed to giving children occasional tokens of recognition (the equivalent of the traditional holy card), not as a bribe, of course, but as a mark of affection!

We believe that sharpening and refining the motivation we offer students is an ongoing task. The more we can sharpen and refine, relying on God's help, the closer we will come to our idea of a school that is Catholic from the inside out.

---

[4] Kohn, *Punished by Rewards*, cites research that indicates that rewards are ineffective in the long run. We found Kohn's analysis of the problem and his review of the research helpful. But as in most of the secular works we have read, there is no concept of a motivational system that looks beyond this world to the life to come.

7.

Pleasure and Eutrapelia In Our School

F OR OUR CORE GROUP, human joy flows from human self-giving. Human self-giving reflects the self-giving of the inner life of the Father, Son, and Holy Spirit. Joy is not the same as pleasure, but joy is often accompanied by pleasure (Christ at the resurrection). Joy is not incompatible with the feeling of pain (Christ on the cross). One of our school songs embodies our approach:

> True joy is the joy of self-giving,
> Whatever the world may say.
> No money or pleasure can give it;
> No sorrow can take it away.

Joy cannot be pursued for its own sake. Joy flows from unselfishness. Unselfishness, for students, means studying hard, being kind to others, obeying the Commandments, accepting the crosses that fall into their lives, and trying to grow in friendship with Christ. The unselfishness and joy children see in their teachers is a powerful encouragement to become less selfish and therefore more full of joy.[1] In all of this, grace plays a prominent part.

Pleasure, when it accompanies joy, is one of God's blessings. We try to introduce pleasure into our school in various ways. Through the rhythm of the church year we vary the experience of school life. There are the quiet days of anticipation and self-denial, and there are the glorious days of celebration and feasts. Schoolchildren take part in parish liturgy, a liturgical life echoed and reflected in the life of the school. There is pleasure in the splendor of Forty Hours, in the intimacy of All Saints, in the light and darkness of Christmas and Easter, in the sweetness of the May devotions. The days of our school year pass by in Technicolor. Very few days have the same hue.

We also provide many opportunities for students to practice the virtue of *eutrapelia*, another name for recreation. *Eutrapelia* is a virtue because it induces pleasure. Pleasure relaxes and prepares the mind and body for the work to come. Sports, Scouts, recess, field days and similar activities come under this virtue. Treating of *eutrapelia*, St. Thomas tells the story of St. John the Evangelist, who when people were scandalized that he was playing a game with his friends, asked one of the questioners to shoot an arrow. When the questioner had shot several arrows, St. John asked him whether he could continue shooting indefinitely. The man answered that if he continued too long, the bow would break. "In like manner the mind would break", replied St. John, "if its tension were never relaxed."[2]

We aim to provide a school atmosphere that leads to joy, containing a proper mixture of pleasure and hard work, even when the hard work entails the cross. We do not intend to teach the children to expect that everything we call upon them to do will be fun. Neither do we intend to be so strict that the atmosphere of the school becomes heavy or inhospitable to

---

[1] "Let us not teach the young to believe they are born into a world of delights and pleasures, but let us strive to enable them to realize that, upon this earth, only the wise and good...can make themselves...at home.... For the healthy man, wealth and happiness would seem to be identical.... But this is delusion, for the...possession of these things has never satisfied a human being." Spalding, *Means and Ends of Education*, p. 16.

[2] Aquinas, *Summa Theologica*, II-II, Q. 168, Art. 2.

wholesome pleasure in the context of Christian joy. We seek a balance, so that our children experience neither indulgence nor deprivation.

8.

From Discipline to Repentance

CHILDREN, LIKE ALL OF US, are affected by original sin. Adam's fault has darkened minds and weakened wills first created, and still remaining, good in their nature. Sometimes children do bad things. They can be mean to their classmates, disrespectful to their teachers, lazy in their schoolwork.

The faults of individuals wound the whole school, and cause disruption in its spiritual life. The wound is not only outward, but inward, because sin slows and restricts the flow of grace. The offender needs restoration to spiritual communion with the body of the school; and the school needs inner, healing grace. Looking to the example of Jesus, our Core Group decided to open a way for healing and reconciliation, not through punishment, but through penitence. Here is how we proceed:

A Climate of Goodness. Our first goal is to sustain a school environment conducive to virtue. Prayer plays the principal part in this sustaining process, along with the good example of the teachers. To encourage the creation of this climate of goodness, students helped to write rules of courtesy.[1]

The school has a firm base of rules and guidelines, not all written down. We try to apply the guidelines with gentleness and respect, and to avoid the multiplication of rules. For example, when students appeared in school with bizarre facial rings, we wrote their parents explaining the historical connection between facial rings and the practice of animism, and asking for the parents' cooperation. When some parents reminded us that there was no rule against multiple facial rings, we responded that there is no rule against necromancy either. We neither intend to make a rule against necromancy nor to permit it in our school. We advised checking with school authorities before sending a child to school with an innovation in appearance. Once parents had accepted this advice, we experienced no further problem.

When Wrongdoing Occurs. Unless offenses are minor enough for the teacher or prefect to handle with a simple reprimand, *general offenses*[2] are referred to our Minister of Repentance, a teacher both highly respected and wise. The minister reviews the written report submitted by the teacher or prefect, speaks kindly to the offender about the love and mercy of Jesus, encourages repentance, and assigns a penance.[3] The penance consists in learning by heart a quotation or a verse of poetry taken from our *Dreaded Book of Memory Exercises*. The memorization takes place at home on the weekend, when

---

[1]   Chapter 10 offers additional details about rules of courtesy. The text of our *Book of Chivalry* will be found in *Appendix A*.

[2]   Here is a partial list of *general offenses*: tardiness; chewing gum; late homework; loitering in halls or lavatories; failure to adhere to dress code; obscene language (written, spoken, or gestured); failure to treat fellow students as Christ; failure to observe bus, car, or safety rules; possession or use of tobacco/alcohol; cheating; disrespect or abuse toward school personnel; disruptive or inappropriate behavior in class; stealing; damage or misuse of school property; falsifying parent signature; leaving school without permission; lying.

[3]   Once a report has been made about a general offense, we do not allow the report or the penance to be questioned. We compare the report to a "call" by a referee. Even if the umpire makes an error, players are expected to accept the decision and get on with the game.

homework is not otherwise expected. The report that goes home to the parents reminds the parents that they have agreed to add something of their own choosing to the penance, and counsels parents to speak to their child in terms of love and repentance. The parents comply, and make a note on the report sheet of what they have added to the penance. The parents return the report sheet to the Minister of Repentance on Monday.

Reports of wrongdoing do not go to the Minister of Repentance on the word of a child, but concern only offenses that teachers and staff have personally observed. We provide reasonable supervision to insure the welfare of the children, but with some exceptions, we do not investigate and resolve all the unobserved injustices that children inflict on one another. We make this policy clear in our *Handbook* and advise parents considering our school not to send their children here if they expect the school to settle all issues among children.[4] Exceptions to this policy occur when the issue is moral turpitude, insult to religion, often-repeated harassment, or danger to life. In such instances, as explained below, we do conduct an investigation, and take the measures mandated by civil and church authorities.

At first we received complaints from parents accustomed to the school's long-standing practice of mediating minor childhood conflicts. But once it became clear from several instances that we were firm in our new policy, parents seemed to relax and modify their expectations.

Replacing the concept of punishment with the Christian ideal of repentance and penance has eliminated the traditional punishments, such as staying after school. Parents, especially those with heavy work schedules, have been grateful, and so have the teachers. Further, because one person handles all general offenses, there is more consistency in the process of repentance within the school.

---

[4] Once we implemented this policy, parental expectations changed, and most parents seemed willing to cooperate. This policy has freed our principal to spend a greater amount of time in the classroom, instead of in the office hearing complaints.

More Serious Issues.   Certain behaviors, whether stemming from wrongdoing or from emotional problems, severely restrict the school's ability to accomplish its purpose. We define these behaviors as follows:

1. A pattern of class disruption demanding so much attention from the teacher that it distracts the teacher from teaching and the class from learning

2. A pattern of class disruption, or a *flagrant act* of insubordination, challenging the authority of the school and giving scandal to others

3. Involvement with drugs or alcohol

4. Offenses relating to weapons

5. Life-threatening acts of violence or threats of the same, whether violence is intended or not

6. Subjecting the Catholic Faith, other Faiths, or human life to ridicule, levity or jest

7. Patterns of unacceptable sexual behavior, or flagrant acts of wrongdoing

8. A *pattern* of harassment of another student

9. Behaviors judged by the school to be equivalent to the above

Instead of invoking suspension or expulsion of the offenders, as diocesan policy permits us to do, we offer a healing process, which for convenience we call the *Red Code.* With our positive encouragement, prayers, and sometimes financial assistance, the process goes forward under the direction of the parents, with the assistance of medical and counseling services the parents select and provide.

In the initial interview with the parents we tell them that John Dewey took a dim view of parents' ability to help their children, but that on the contrary, we have the utmost confidence in them! We then review with them a written statement containing our analysis of the problem and the six-step process which is required.

The six steps are:

1. Conviction of guilt
2. Repentance and purpose of amendment
3. Proof of sincerity and penance
4. Steps to seek God's forgiveness
5. Conviction of dependence on God and steps to obtain His mercy
6. Forgiving others and asking their forgiveness

The school provides criteria for judging that the child has successfully completed each stage of the process. The school also decides whether the process is to be carried out in the "schooling-at-home mode" or in the "in-school" mode. (The primary consideration is the effect that the presence of the child will have on the ability of the school to meet its daily educational objectives.)

During the process, the school does not relate directly to the child, but is in regular contact with parents; and if parents desire, with counselors and doctors. Working together, school and parents assess the child's progress through the six steps. By mutual agreement they determine when the process of healing has been successfully completed.

During the first year of the new policy, we had five *red codes*. The incidents concerned jokes about suicide, Columbine-type threats of violence (in jest), and patterns of classroom disruption. When invited to lead their children through the six-step healing process, parents were most cooperative, and were grateful for the school's support. All five *red code* incidents were resolved successfully the first year, and there has hardly been an occurrence since.

9.

Creating Nostalgia

W H E N   W E   L I S T E N E D to old-timers talking about our school on the occasion of its seventy-fifth anniversary, we were struck by the stories they told. Some stories were about teachers and escapades. But mostly the alumni spoke about beautiful religious experiences the school had provided that remained in memory all these years, moments recalled with nostalgia: the May procession, the Forty Hours, the drama of Tenebrae. These experiences had impressed them and in important ways colored their lives.

These reminiscences made our Core Group do an inventory of experiences our school offers that have the potential of coloring children's lives. Here is what we found.

General Experiences. We offer the religious exercises customary in Catholic schools: weekly Mass, occasional class Masses, the Sacrament of Penance during Advent and Lent, Stations of the Cross, May Devotions, volunteer prayer groups during lunch break, opportunity for individuals to visit the Blessed Sacrament during recess, Confirmation retreat.

Grade-by-Grade Experiences. The second graders experience the loving preparation for First Penance and First Communion. This is a time of deep spirituality for them and for their parents. We try to make it as holy as possible and to concentrate on what is important. But we have a party too!

The third, fourth, and fifth graders are privileged to come to the closing of Forty Hours, honoring the Presence of Our Lord among us. A sense of excitement and anticipation pervades the school as Forty Hours approaches. The coordinator of the feast gives inspirational talks, and lights appear in the trees of the Liturgical Quadrangle to announce to the neighborhood that Forty Hours is coming. On the appointed days there are class retreats and visits to the Blessed Sacrament, and many children attend the evening devotions with their parents. But on the final night the third, fourth and fifth graders participate in the outdoor procession, along with the rest of the congregation. The procession is spectacular, with Knights of Columbus, Kohathites (high school servers) in their red cassocks, all the regular servers and Eucharistic Ministers. Under a red and gold baldachino the celebrant carries the Blessed Sacrament encased in a splendid monstrance. The procession follows a path outlined with luminaries, to the accompaniment of an ensemble (symphony orchestra members), drums, bells, and incense. Adults who have participated for many years are still moved by this popular devotion. We hope the children will remember it with pleasure too. And, oh yes, after the celebration there are ice cream cones for the children!

The sixth graders participate in Tenebrae on Wednesday of Holy Week. Vespers, conducted in darkness, is accompanied by sung Lamentations. The children extinguish the candles representing the apostles one by one deserting the Lord in His agony. And at the end there is a loud noise (clamor) as the Christ candle is put out. Sixth Graders are especially good at making noise, and this responsibility puts them to the test.

The seventh graders do a Good Friday Trope, a simple version of a passion play, complete with costumes, lights and narratives.

The eighth graders assist in the extensive preparations for the Easter Vigil; they serve as ushers and candle-lighters at the Vigil itself; and afterward the eighth grade hosts a party for the new Catholics, whom they try to make welcome in our parish.

Service. The school does not conduct service projects as such, but offers inspiration and guidance. Once a year the parish volunteer coordinator visits the classrooms to promote awareness of opportunities for service in parish and community. Opportunities in the parish include: serving Mass, children's choir, playing instruments at liturgies, helping prepare for special feasts, nursery aide, baby-sitting for parents involved in meetings, brass polishing in church (second, third, fourth grade), helping at parish parties and the Parish Fair. Eighth graders may join the Kohathites (high school servers); help prepare a monthly dinner for the poor and conduct the annual Christmas party; serve as lectors, ushers or members of the adult choir; and join the high school Youth Group, which does periodic service projects. We support and encourage young people who wish to initiate and lead new parish projects and activities. In addition, there are volunteer opportunities in the community, such as hospital service, nursing home assistance, and Scout service projects. Almost all students choose to participate in some form of volunteer service.

Missions. Students are encouraged to make sacrifices for the missions and to contribute money and prayers for the preaching of the gospel and for the poor.

Prayer Partners. Older students adopt younger students as prayer partners, and help the younger students in various ways. In addition, the second graders "adopt" the parish babies born that year, and keep in touch with them through birthday cards and prayers year by year. Thus when these children enroll in school, there is an old friend in eighth grade to welcome them.

Seminarians.   Each year a nearby seminary assigns theological students to help with the teaching of religion. The seminarians mix with the students, play sports with them, and answer their questions about seminary life.

Pastor's Conferences.   There is a pastoral conference with each student in seventh and eighth grade each year. Conferences focus on prayer and student interests, and provide an opportunity for questions about the spiritual life.

An Opportunity to Choose Priorities.   We offer children an opportunity to make religion a priority in their lives. We are not resigned to letting them think that religious exercises are what you do if you have time left over from the "really important" things of life.

Here are some examples.   The date established by our diocese for the closing of Forty Hours often conflicts with our town's Trick-or-Treat night. Third, fourth, and fifth graders are expected to be at church on that night. Most parents are willing to create enthusiasm for Forty Hours by word and example, and to encourage their children to make this sacrifice for love of Jesus in the Blessed Sacrament. Some, however, objected and did not bring their children to church. The principal wrote a courteous letter to these parents expressing disappointment for an opportunity missed.   Nothing further was said, but the following year all the children were present.

A second incident concerned Holy Week.   The original intent of a school holiday on Good Friday was to give families the opportunity of celebrating the Triduum together.   We discovered, however, that during this most sacred time families were taking their children to Disney World.   We decided, therefore, to offer the children religious experiences of various types on Holy Thursday, Good Friday, and (for the eighth grade) Holy Saturday; and to begin the spring holiday on Easter Tuesday.   Since we clearly explained this plan in our *Handbook* and since the Lenten program heightened their sense of excitement, most parents expressed support for the new program.

Some parents, however, objected strongly, and refused to send their children to school on Good Friday. We let the matter pass, but could sense that the parental issue was one of priorities. Parents did not subsequently discuss the matter with us, but after two years, the new policy is firmly in place, and parents now plan to take their vacations during the free days after Easter.

The local public school district provides bus service to our school. Although we are grateful for this service, we resolved not to let it tyrannize us. If the busses are not running on a day when we want our children in school for religious purposes, parents find other ways to send their children, usually by car-pooling. As one parent remarked, "We bring the children to athletic events all the time. There is no reason why we cannot bring them to school occasionally to accommodate the school's religious schedule."

10.

School Manners for Teachers, Children, and Parents

W E   E X P E C T   T E A C H E R S to treat children with courtesy and respect. Children are created in God's image; they have been redeemed by Jesus Christ; they are born again in baptism; they are destined some day to enjoy the vision of the Father, Son, and Holy Spirit in heaven. Even though weakened by original sin and subject to sin like the rest of us, they have great dignity, and are worthy of respect.

Respect implies not only kindness, but also challenge. Calling children to do their best, according to the talents God has given them, best enhances their dignity as children. When children find it difficult to respond, teachers offer every encouragement, making their expectations clear and resisting the temptation to indulge children for the sake of fleeting favor.

Children. When we began our project, the Core Group found that courtesy among our school children left much to be desired. In many cases, children were rude to one another, and to their teachers. What we decided to do was to seek their collaboration in a year-long process of writing a book of manners. The various classes, with the teachers' encouragement, held discussions on courtesy and formulated rules. When a class had come to agreement on a rule, that rule was placed on a computer banner in the hall for all to read. Other classes could then readily discuss, add to, or revise the rule. During the year, a noticeable improvement in the general school climate showed in increased acts of courtesy. After a year of discussion, the banners, collected and grouped into categories for publication, proclaimed chivalry in class, chivalry on the playground, chivalry toward grown-ups, chivalry in sports, chivalry in church, chivalry at table. At the end of the year the teachers noticed substantial growth in courtesy, especially on the playground. The complete text of *Our Book of Chivalry* will be found in *Appendix A*.

Parents. Most parents relate courteously to our school. But we thought it helpful to provide guidelines, in order to make clear what we expect.

Our *first* concern was to clarify our policy on certain vital issues. We expect parents to contact us immediately regarding incidents of (1) moral turpitude, (2) insult to religion, (3) often-repeated harassment by any member of the school, or (4) danger to life. In addition to action by the school, some of these matters require recourse to civil or church authorities.

Our *second* concern was to offer advice for those who need to make complaints. We published the following leaflet:

How to Complain with Courtesy

There is nothing wrong with complaining. How else will wrongs be righted, mistakes corrected, and truth be known? There is a difference, however, between making a complaint and being complainer. A complainer is often too regular in criticism, too intolerant of human weakness, and too ready to presume the worst. Making a complaint in a Christian and courteous manner requires finesse and kindness. Here are some suggestions.

1. *Deal with your anger before you make your complaint.* Calm down. You may be right, but you may also be wrong. Don't burn the bridges of future relationships by venting anger against the person to whom you are complaining. Use your therapist for that purpose. School personnel do not have to put up with venting; it's not in their contract.

2. *Clarify the purpose of your complaint.* What are your short-term and long-term objectives? What do you wish changed, avoided, corrected? Are you looking for friendly cooperation on solving a problem? Would you like to see a new policy? Have you asked yourself if complaining is the best way of accomplishing your purpose, or if perhaps there might be a better way?

3. *Give careful attention to the tone of your complaint and the assumptions behind it.* Don't speak so that the person listening to you will perceive what you say like this: "This person is telling me that I am incompetent, and is questioning my word."

4. *Make notes.* Even if you make your complaint verbally, it is a good idea to write out beforehand what you intend to say. Writing helps you examine your assumptions and to search for the most courteous approach.

It is our hope not only to teach Christian ideals to children, but to demonstrate to them how adults put these ideals into practice. The way we relate to one another in highly-charged circumstances gives us a prime opportunity of doing that very thing.

Our *third* concern was to establish the following guidelines about child-to-child offenses.

When Children Complain about One Another

1. When the child reports something related to the four issues mentioned above--moral turpitude, insult to religion, often-repeated harassment, or danger to life or limb--contact the school authorities immediately. We will investigate.

2. The Ministry of Repentance handles conflicts that teachers or prefects personally observe among children. Except for the four areas mentioned above, the school does not investigate or resolve unobserved injustices that children perpetrate on one another. We expect parents to deal with these issues themselves, through recourse to Scripture: "Love one another" (Jn 13:34). "If you do not forgive others, neither will your Father forgive you your offenses" (Mt 6:14). "To no one render evil for evil, but provide good things not only in the sight of God, but also in the sight of all men" (Rom 12:17). "Love your enemies" (Lk 6:27). "Bless those who persecute you" (Rom 12:15).

3. If a child is being left out of a peer group, parents are advised to enlist the aid of a counselor to help the child work through the problem. Friendship cannot be forced, but learning better relational skills may help a child become more readily accepted. For our part, we try to address the root of the *clique* problem by creating a Christian atmosphere of love and openness to all.

Our *fourth* concern was to offer specific guidance on children's complaints about teachers. In a day when every movie and every television show downplay authority, children need to learn, at home and in school, to give authority proper respect. Teaching proper respect for authority has always been a prominent feature of Catholic schools.

When Children Complain about Teachers

1. When what the child reports at home involves moral turpitude, insult to religion, often-repeated harassment, or immediate danger to life, contact the school authorities immediately.

2. Otherwise, take the complaint with a grain of salt. Children, however sincere and truthful, do not always perceive what the teacher says or does--and the *context* in which it is said or done--in a totally accurate manner. This kind of misperception occurs most often if the teacher has displeased the child by offering correction or requiring hard work.

3. Presume that the teacher acted wisely. Like parents, teachers are committed to doing their best. Teachers are not always able to do or say the most perfect thing on the spur of the moment. But neither are parents. Allow a margin of error.

4. In light of the above, side with the teacher, not the child. That way you will show your love for your child in the long run, even though you may displease the child in the short run. Some day your child will thank you for teaching an important lesson.

5. Tell your child that you expect him or her to obey the teacher, without hesitation, and without asking "Why?" The teacher is the authority, and the child is the learner.

6. Do not expect the school to ask the teacher to offer explanations. It is not good for children to have the power of requiring teachers to explain themselves.

As one might expect, there were a few incidents the first year. After that, however, our policy became part of the school's culture, and the previous custom of frequent minor complaints virtually disappeared.

11.

The Outside of the Cup

W<small>E DID NOT SPEND MUCH TIME</small> discussing the physical environment of our school, not because we thought it unimportant, but because it seemed to require less attention than other elements.

Our school is well maintained and cheerful, but old-fashioned and somewhat cramped. We do have the use of a large parish gymnasium and stage, in a separate building. The Liturgical Quadrangle surrounded by tall trees, and the grassy playing field, offer relief from our paved playground area. The art class painted a mural of trees, in the style of Fra Angelico, on the side of the pastor's garage. This mural, along with outdoor benches, enhances the open area. Vigorously enforced security and safety measures are in place.

As time and money become available, we would like to place more quality art in the public areas of the school. We have some good art now, but our collection always has room for improvement. We would like the children to study in an environment of good art, both old and new.

12.

Fighting Pelagianism

Our core group determined to do everything possible to express our trust in God, and to combat the Pelagian idea that we can succeed by our efforts, rather than by cooperation with grace. We gave attention to the following issues: prayer, removing the dark cloud, not trying to do too much, and keeping down the cost.

Prayer. There was already much prayer in the school, for example, first thing in the morning, and before each class. To add to this, we composed a new school prayer, which embodied many ideas of the renewal, and which the principal inserted into various school activities. Here is the prayer:

> Lord, Jesus Christ ...
> Make us seekers of the truth as it actually is,
> not as the world tells us it is.
>
> Give us help in our school work, because clever-
> ness alone will not prepare us to help You

create the new heavens and the new earth.

When being good and working hard are not fun,
teach us how to sacrifice, so that we may carry
out Your beautiful Will.

Help us to see You in others, even those we do
not like, and help us to treat others as we
would treat You.

Receive all our good deeds, join them to Your
sacrifice at the Mass, to the glory of God and
the good of all the world.

Keep us from sin, and bring us some day into
Your company, along with the Father and the Holy
Spirit, forever and ever. Amen.

We were pleased that students occasionally quoted phrases from the prayer during conferences and classes. We hope that constant repetition will bring grace down upon the school.[1]

Dispersing the Dark Cloud. When a new pastor came to our parish, he noted a cloud of sin hanging over the school. The children were not attending Sunday Mass. Several years before the renewal process began, we made a major effort to remove the dark cloud and release the flow of God's grace. As a parish we

---

[1]   A book of prayer for children is in preparation. We are considering the following prayers: Prayer before a Game, Prayer When in a Bad Mood, Prayer for Offering Myself at Mass, Prayer When Brothers and Sisters are a Pain, Prayer for Help in Doing Hard Things, Prayer when I Have to Do Something Hard, Prayer before Babysitting, Prayer before a Party, Prayer before Going to the Mall, Prayer before Exams, Prayer after Having Been Mean to Others, Prayer for Forgiveness for Gossip, Prayer for Our Country, Prayer for Choosing a Calling Life, Prayer When Concerned about What People Think of Me.

acted on our belief that without the grace of God nothing is really accomplished. Here is what we did.

The pastor gave eleven homilies on the beauty of the Mass and the privilege of standing before God in worship. He stressed the concept of public sacrifice, and reminded the congregation that we come to Mass not only to *get something out of it*, but to *give ourselves to God*.

The school made sure that the children knew that Sunday Mass was not only a great privilege, but a strict obligation.[2] We discovered that the children already knew this; the problem was they were not doing it.

There was wide consultation on the issue within the parish, including the Pastoral Advisory Council, the School Committee, leaders of all youth organizations, school staff and other leaders. There was firm support for addressing the problem.

Our first task was to make sure that adults appointed to be role models for our young people were giving good example by attending Mass. We developed detailed policy, outlining the expectations for teachers, CCD, Scouts, coaches, Youth Group leaders, and the like. For the most part we received full and enthusiastic cooperation from the leaders. Each year we asked our 150 youth leaders to sign an *Assurance Statement*, after which we published their names in the Parish Bulletin, along with expressions of appreciation. At first there were two or three uncooperative leaders, who were a cross to the officers of the organizations they served. The officers loyally backed the pastor's decision that the offending leaders were to resign. The experience, although painful, was a spiritual gain.

At Easter the Parish Bulletin carried a pastoral letter, entitled, *Our Very Own Earthquake*. The statement was a call to make the Sacred Liturgy the source and summit of the Christian life. God cares for those who do not participate in public

---

[2]   We worked from the *Catechism of the Catholic Church*: "The Sunday Eucharist is the foundation and confirmation of all Christian practice. For this reason the faithful are obliged to participate in the Eucharist on days of obligation, unless excused for a serious reason (for example illness, the care of infants) or dispensed by their own pastor. Those who deliberately fail in this obligation commit a grave sin." [2181]

worship, and calls them to repentance. We will do our part by offering home-style retreats, called the Ananias Program, for the religious instruction of families not coming to Mass. Children who wish to be enrolled in our school, however, must attend Mass. If parents are not willing to bring their children to church personally, but wish them to be enrolled in the school, parents may sign a *Sponsor Contract* authorizing a grandparent or a friend to bring them to Mass. That way no child need be excluded.

The pastoral letter was quite extensive, developing these and other points at length. The tone was positive and encouraging, but it made clear that the pastor would implement the new policy with tenacity and persistence. After the announcement, a leaflet explaining the new policy was published. The leaflet was distributed to parents and parishioners, and was available in the church vestibule.

What happened then? Nothing. There was no improvement in Mass attendance.

First Communion was scheduled several weeks after the announcement. The pastor wrote to the parents of the First Communicants inviting them to a pastoral conference *for the good of their souls.* He scheduled conferences with each family at fifteen minute intervals. In this informal setting, the pastor spoke to the parents about their eternal salvation, and encouraged them in a positive manner to give good example to their children by bringing them to Mass. Bringing a child to Mass would, in fact, be a requirement for the child's First Communion. Most parents seemed embarrassed by their laxity, and readily agreed to reform their religious practice. Of the thirty sets of parents, only one left the school and the parish, and only one threatened the pastor (fortunately an empty threat).

At this time, the teachers began to ask the First Communicants every Monday to state that they attended Sunday Mass, or if not, why not (sickness, and the like). In a little prayer ceremony, the First Communicants received their first envelope boxes. From now on they were to place an envelope in the Sunday collection containing a sacrificial offering from their allowance, or if their parents provided them no allowance or money for church, they could record on the envelope one of their good deeds.

With a great deal of encouragement, Mass attendance began gradually to increase. By the end of the school year, we were ready to require parents of children who wished to enroll or re-register their children in the school to sign our *Memorandum of Understanding.* After the first year we required this memorandum only for new students

Memorandum of Agreement

TO: Pastor   RE: New Student

We promise and intend to fulfill the requirements stated in No. 701 of the school *Handbook* regarding church attendance. We clearly understand that these are conditions upon which our child is to be admitted to our school, and/or is to be permitted to remain there.

If our child is a CATHOLIC, we intend . . .

1. That our child, will attend Mass each week on Sunday, and on Holy Days of obligation, from the age of seven; and will, with rare exceptions, attend in the parish in which registered. From the beginning of Second Grade, the child will turn in a weekly envelope at Mass, submitting a good deed, a monetary offering, or both. (We monitor Mass attendance through the envelope system. Students from other Catholic parishes must furnish an annual testimonial from their pastors that they are attending Mass.)

2. If prevented by work schedules, or other serious reasons from bringing our child to the parish of registration on a regular

weekly basis, we will take the initiative in conferring with the pastor to arrange for a sponsor to fulfill this obligation.[3]

3. If custody arrangements interfere with No. 1, we will take the initiative in conferring with the pastor to see what should be done.

4. The Catholic parent (or parents) whose name is signed below will give good example by coming regularly to Mass on Sundays and Holy Days of obligation, at the parish in which registered, unless legitimately excused, and will use envelopes.

If our child is an ECUMENICAL student, he (she) will attend, on a regular basis, the church in which our family is registered. A letter of attestation from our pastor is required for enrollment, and may be requested by the school at other times.

[Signature and date]

* * *

Through the years, we monitored Mass attendance through the envelope system. Staff conducted reviews in November, March, and August. If a pattern of laxity appeared, the pastor conferred with the parents. Most of the time parents agreed to do better, and we let the matter drop. Only rarely has it been necessary, after appropriate warnings, to tell parents that their children will not be re-registered in the fall.

By the time we were ready to undertake the renewal process we describe in this book, the children of our school were generally attending Sunday Mass. It was a relief to us to know that the dark cloud had been lifted from our school, and that grace, joy, and serenity seemed to be flowing much more abundantly than before. It was quite evident to us that whatever

---

[3] In the first year we had four children who needed sponsors because their parents were not at that point in their lives where they were ready to go to church. The sponsors were grandparents. The arrangement worked out very well.

success we experienced came from God's gracious goodness rather than from our own human effort.

Not Trying to Do Too Much. Our diocese determines curriculum. Curriculum includes the basics, plus other subject matter, in line with the Catholic school tradition.[4] From the mid-nineteenth century there had been pressure to expand the curriculum of the public school. But when John Dewey articulated his theory that children should learn from all of life,[5] the curriculum began to expand, and continues to escalate to this day. The prevailing assumption seems to be that the school is to address more and more of society's issues and problems. There has also been a trend to move more and more extracurricular activities into the curriculum.

There was much talk at this time about offering classes, retreats, and spiritual direction to parents. While we agreed that the need was there, we took the position that the parish should take on this function, instead of the school. The parish began to offer mini-courses to parents on Sunday mornings, and various retreat experiences. The response was not as great as expected, but the parish is committed to continuing and expanding its efforts.

Our school does not offer counseling; we do not put the cost of offering therapy into the tuition budget. Counseling, however, is available through Catholic Charities at a modest cost. The parish offers financial assistance if needed.

At the time of the renewal, there was pressure to send students to a neighboring school for a course in high school algebra. We decided not to send students out for algebra, because we needed all our class time to bring our students up to standard in the subjects our diocese prescribes for elementary schools.

---

[4] We were instructed on this historical point by Curtis, *Educating the Faithful*, p. 84.

[5] Dewey, *School and Society*, pp. 181 ff.

We are careful not to adopt an expansionist mentality. We have a clear idea of what our elementary school needs to do,[6] and we do not wish to attempt so much that there is not enough time for that priority.

Keeping Down the Cost.   We discussed at length the temptation we experienced to compete with the public school, and we prayed for grace and guidance. Subjects and activities that might seem standard in the public system, from our perspective may appear as frills.

We have few frills in our school, and that for two reasons. We want to use available money to upgrade teachers' salaries. We want to keep the cost of tuition low enough that people of ordinary means will be able to send their children to our school.

One issue that caused much pain was the hot lunch. Hot lunch is currently limited to a simple Friday meal brought in from the outside. For the sake of convenience,[7] many parents would like us to install a kitchen, and provide a regular staff to cook a hot meal daily. Out of affection for parents and children, we really wanted to accommodate them, and studied the issue in careful detail. When we looked into the real cost of running such a program, including the administration involved in hiring, supervising, accounting, and complying with state requirements, we regretfully concluded that we could not add this program without compromising the time and energy the principal now spends in classroom supervision. Without an increase in personnel, and a consequent rise in tuition, we cannot add even one more item of administrative paperwork to what is already required.

Naturally we are saddened when Catholic parents choose the public school over our school; but we have come to terms with it. We are not anxious. We do what we believe we are called to do, leaving the rest in the hands of God.

---

[6]   More about this priority in Chapters 13 and 14.

[7]   We are not in a situation where children would have nothing to eat if the school did not provide lunch.

13.

Basics Plus

Knowledge That Contributes to Human Dignity

OURS IS AN ELEMENTARY SCHOOL, kindergarten to eighth grade. In the Catholic view, all education is supposed to enhance the dignity of the human person.[1] That enhancement, however, has different goals at different levels--elementary, secondary, advanced. Our Core Group has become aware that, even among Thomists,[2] there is more than one approach to secondary and advanced education. We are not qualified to judge the merit of these approaches; but we are convinced that the fundamentals we teach in our elementary school provide a good basis for whatever is to come.

An education built on sand detracts from human dignity. Think of the graduate student unable to write a grammatical sentence. Or the young child encouraged to be creative by banging on the piano before learning the notes. Or the dignitary giving a speech laced with grammatical errors that should have been corrected in fifth grade.

---

[1] Maritain, *Crossroads*, p. 25; Cunningham, *Pivotal Problems*, p. 556.

[2] A sampling of variations in approach will be found in McInerny, *Common Things*.

It is the goal of our elementary school therefore, to teach those basic language, computational, and religious facts, ideas, and skills that the dignity of every person requires. We teach more than these basics, of course, in accordance with the diocesan curriculum approved by our bishop. But we have a special interest in making sure that graduates of our school are well provided with foundational knowledge.[3]

We knew we could not examine every element of the curriculum, so we first looked at the results of the Iowa Tests[4] given to every Catholic student in our diocese. In Fifth and Eighth Grade, tests compare cognitive ability with achievement. In our school, achievement and ability were found to be consonant.

Composite achievement scores[5] were satisfactory, but we noted that the sub-scores for mathematical computation[6] were low. We asked the teachers to give special attention to this area, and reemphasized our policy that calculators were not to substitute for human effort. The teachers responded faithfully, and scores rose substantially during the next two years.

Grammar sub-scores were also adequate, but the test did not provide a clear picture of our local situation, where grammatical errors in speech patterns are common. Our children's speech reflected these local patterns and carried over into their written compositions.[7]

---

[3] Ravitch, *Left Back*, pp. 17, 460.

[4] In trying to understand what the Iowa Tests tell us, we read the manuals provided by the publisher, Riverside, and also reviewed a standard text on testing: John Salvia and James E. Ysseldyke, *Assessment* (Houghton Mifflin, 1995).

[5] Composite scores include vocabulary, reading comprehension, spelling, capitalization, punctuation, usage, mathematical concepts, data interpretation, social studies, science, reference materials, mathematical computation.

[6] Adding, subtracting, multiplying, dividing.

[7] Charlemagne, conscious of poor speech patterns in his realm, obtained the services of Alcuin, not only as his own teacher, but to spread enthusiasm for grammar throughout the Frankish Kingdom. Roger Collins, *Charlemagne* (University of Toronto, 1998), p. 120. Charlemagne was worried about the decline of civilization, and so are we.

Our objectives, therefore, were to give students competence in using the parts of speech; familiarity with sentence structure; knowledge of the rules of syntax, usage, capitalization and punctuation; skill in spelling; and the ability to write sentences and paragraphs without grammatical errors.   All of these elements were called for in our diocesan syllabus, and were included in the language arts textbooks we were using.[8] In the classroom, however, these elements were being *covered* rather than *learned*.

The selection of teaching methods for achieving these objectives was, of course, in the hands of the teachers. But we did warn teachers about John Dewey's intimidating attack on distributed practice (drill). Distributed practice is an important doorway into the memory, provided such drill is employed in the right way. We also pointed out that when coaches really wanted their students to learn strategies for winning basketball games, coaches resorted to teaching by means of diagrams. Can the same tactic apply to learning sentence structure?

How can we make sure that the children actually learn, that is, understand and remember, their grammar? We decided not to use tests and grades, but to use Grammar Games. Grammar Games are like War Games.   The army's purpose is preparedness; our purpose is knowledge.

We hold one Grammar Game in September, to assess what children retain over the summer. And we hold another in March, to determine the specific things we need to teach individual children before the end of the school year.[9]

A game consists in writing answers to a number of questions designed to demonstrate the students' knowledge. The questions cover *all* the material pupils are supposed to know at their grade level. Questions are posed in a homey format, but a format not conducive to guessing. Students also write a brief

---

[8] *World of Language* (Silver Burdett & Ginn).

[9] Theoretically we can send the children to summer school, if they have not mastered everything by the end of the year. Fortunately, implementing this option has not yet become necessary.

composition to demonstrate grammatically correct writing and good penmanship. Since Grammar Games take some time, these Grammar Games are extended over a two-day period.

The student results are not graded, but errors in answering the questions are circled in red and counted for each child. When we began the Grammar Games only forty-three percent of the questions received correct answers. Our teachers worked hard, and accepted the games as a challenge. Reinforced by spiritual motivation, most students showed gradual improvement. After two years, ninety-two percent of the questions were answered correctly. Although much remains to be done, we are pleased with the results to date. We are hearing fewer and fewer expressions on the playground such as, "I don't want no applesauce."

There were several other things we asked the teachers to do. One was to encourage the children to do as much writing as possible, stressing accuracy. We hope that accuracy will become second nature as the students move along into creative writing in the upper grades and beyond.

The students participate in our annual extracurricular Reading for the Kingdom program: this program runs from November to April. In the first year, eighth graders read an average of twelve books; by the third year the average had increased to sixteen. The whole school read 8,445 books the first year; by the third year, the total had increased to 13,507.

We asked the teachers to give the children practice in reading out loud. We also specified that poetry be included in the curriculum. We directed the teachers to teach the children good penmanship. Children learn touch typing in computer class, but we require the students to submit homework and class assignments in good handwriting. In eighth grade, students may submit assignments using word processing, but not in the lower grades.

Finally, we committed the school to teaching computer literacy by the time of graduation. As our diocese specifies, computer literacy includes computer operations, word processing, database, spreadsheet, e-mail and fax. Students also learn internet access, search techniques and computer ethics.

Many children have already learned these skills at home by the time we are ready to teach them in school.[10]

---

[10] We are currently giving careful study to the uses of computers as instructional aids, and have begun to examine the literature on both sides of this complex issue.

14.

Teaching Religion in a Culture Where Truth is Relative

Our school's ultimate purpose is to give glory to God, by helping children come closer to Him.[1] We do this in two ways: indirectly by providing a Christian setting for children six and one-half hours a day; directly by what we teach.

Knowledge can enhance children's potential to glorify God. Some knowledge is of a general nature, for example, mathematics and science; such knowledge increases the individual's capacity for building the earthly city and the Kingdom of God. Other knowledge focuses directly on religion, bringing children to the understanding of God, His plan for us, and His moral precepts. Love of God does not necessarily flow

---

[1]   When we speak of "educating the whole person", we do not mean that such education will be fully accomplished in class. Children also obtain knowledge and grow into Christian commitment in retreats, in the everyday life of good Catholic families, in the parish and school setting, and in other religious groups.

from knowledge about Him, but knowledge can certainly extend our capacity for love. You cannot love what you do not know.[2]

The focus of our religion classes is knowledge.[3] This focus does not mean that we limit our teachings to "propositions".

> There are three persons in one God.
> Jesus Christ is God and man.
> Marriage is a Sacrament.

In line with the modern catechetical renewal,[4] we try to align our teaching toward a "response in Faith".

> The self-giving of the three Persons is reflected in
>   the joy we experience in giving ourselves in
>   service to others.
> It is Jesus who loves us so much that He died to
>   Redeem us.

---

[2] Aquinas, *Summa Theologica*, I, Q.82, Art.3; I-II, Q. 10, Art.1. We profited greatly in our thinking on this point by: Donald J. Reitz, *Moral Crisis in the Schools: What Parents and Teachers Need to Know* (Cathedral, 1998), pp. 93-113.

[3] In *The Religious Dimension of Education in a Catholic School* (Congregation for Catholic Education, 1988), the Church affirms the importance of religious knowledge, and points out that there is a difference in classroom teaching in school and non-school settings. We note that G. Rossiter has treated this point in "The Need for a 'Creative Distance' between Catechetics and Religious Education in Catholic Schools", *Religious Education* (77), pp. 21-40. We would not want to say that religious knowledge tends to get crowded out of non-school catechetical programs. But we are ready to affirm emphatically that the school provides a precious opportunity for children to acquire religious knowledge. This is one of the reasons why we are so enthusiastic about Catholic schools.

[4] Francis D. Kelly, *The Mystery We Proclaim: Catechesis at the Third Millennium* (Our Sunday Visitor, 1993), pp. 9-25.

> Marriage is a created reflection of the self-image
> Of the mutual self-giving of the Father, Son, and
> Holy Spirit.

We do not expect an *immediate* faith response to what we present in class. The response may come later in life when people, having understood and remembered our teaching, can find added meaning, amid the buffetings of experience, in what we have taught. We hope to teach in such a way that the knowledge children obtain in our school will serve as a firm foundation for their response in faith, not only here and now, but in adult life.

We use our classroom time for teaching our students what they need to know, including moral knowledge, without undue anxiety about evoking an immediate response. In our view, the opportunity for systematic religious instruction on a daily basis is one of the most attractive features of our school.

We are also careful to include in our classroom teaching things that are important, but not central to the Christian message.

> The requirements for a valid marriage.
> The laws of fast and abstinence.

The bulk of our classroom teaching of religion follows the diocesan syllabus and approved texts, and employs a variety of pedagogical methods, including the (knowledge-oriented) experiential approaches.

Our Core Group decided to supplement this subject matter in two ways: providing a tool box of religious definitions; and addressing the problem of teaching religion to children growing up in a relativistic culture.

A Tool Box of Catholic Definitions

Even before we began the renewal process, our parish had offered children a tool box of fifty-four Catholic definitions, adapted from the *Catechism of the Catholic Church*, to learn by heart, at the rate of six per year from kindergarten to eighth grade. We did not view this small tool box as a course in Catholic doctrine (as formerly people perhaps viewed the *Baltimore Catechism*), or even as a complete set of definitions, but as a handy aid to present understanding and future study.

In providing this tool box we did not let John Dewey's hostility to memorization intimidate us. Rather we adopted the positive view of Pope John Paul II,[5] and that of the *National Catechetical Directory*.[6] Memorization has a proper place in the handing on of the faith.

The full text of our booklet, *Some Catholic Definitions That Children May Learn by Heart* is contained in *Appendix B*. Here are the fifty-four questions:

---

[5]   "We are all aware that this method [memorization] can present certain disadvantages, not the least of which is that it lends itself to insufficient ... assimilation, reducing all knowledge to formulas that are repeated without being properly understood. These disadvantages ... have in some places led to the almost complete suppression--according to some, alas, the definitive suppression--of memorization in catechesis.... The blossoms, if we may call them that, of faith and piety do not grow in the desert places of a memory-less catechesis. What is essential is that the texts that are memorized must at the same time be taken in and gradually understood in depth, in order to become a source of Christian life." (John Paul II, *Catechesi Tradendae*, n. 55)

[6] "While catechesis cannot be limited to the repetition of formulas and it is essential that formulas and facts pertaining to faith be understood, memorization has nevertheless had a special place in the handing-on of the faith throughout the ages and should continue to have such a place today." *National Catechetical Directory*, p. 176.

K. Kindergarten. Sign of the Cross. Angel of God. Hail Mary. Grace before Meals.

1. First Grade. Who made us? Why did God make us? What does God call us to do? What do we mean by the Blessed Trinity? Which are the three persons of the Blessed Trinity? The Lord's Prayer. Glory to the Father.

2. Second Grade. Who is Jesus Christ? Why did Jesus suffer on the cross? Act of Contrition. How do we share in the cross of Jesus? (The Mass)

3. Third Grade. What is the Church? Who founded the Church? Why did Jesus Christ found the Church? Who are the pastors of the Church? Who is the pope? Who are the bishops? Apostles' Creed.

4. Fourth Grade. What is faith? What is hope? What is charity? What are the ten commandments? What is prayer? What is sin? What is mortal sin? What is venial sin? Act of Contrition.

5. Fifth Grade. What are Sacraments? What is grace? What is sanctifying grace? What is actual grace? Name the Sacraments. What is Baptism? What is Confirmation? What is the Eucharist? How is Jesus offered in sacrifice in the Eucharist? What is the Sacrament of Penance?

6. Sixth Grade. What is perfect contrition? What is imperfect contrition?

7. Seventh Grade. What is Anointing of the Sick? What is Holy Orders? What is Matrimony?

8. Eighth Grade. How does the Gospel of Jesus Christ reach us today? What is the New Testament? What happens to each of us at death? After judgment, what happens to us? What is heaven? What is hell? What is purgatory? What is the resurrection of the body?

We asked parents to teach their children these definitions at home, and to explain them thoroughly. For parents who did not understand the concepts, we offered classes and private instructions. Many found teaching their children a helpful review of their own religious knowledge. Some children found memorization extremely difficult, even traumatic, perhaps as a result of having been frequently subjected to a multiplicity of rapid-fire images on the television and elsewhere. The first year saw loud protests, and two families even left the parish. By the second year, however, the children began to take pride in their ability to learn by heart, and the objections subsided.

The process is this. Children and parents have copies of our booklet containing all the definitions. In February we asked parents to give their children a written test at home. We expected children to write the answers to the questions for their present grade level, as well as for the previous grades. Parents sign this pre-test, and return it to the teachers, thus qualifying their children to take the test in class. Tests are not graded, but mistakes are circled. Teachers then work with individual children, until children know the circled definitions by the end of the year.

Learning the Catholic definitions by heart has become an accepted part of school life. In our archives we have boxes of tests that show, year by year, fewer and fewer mistakes on the tests. Teachers reported that having a tool box of definitions made it easier for children to understand the regular religious subject matter taught in class.

The Culture Factor

Children, from birth, must confront a culture of false ideals ("slimy principles"), a culture that warps their ability to understand. For example:

Subjectivism: What I think is true, is true for me.

Pelagianism: I do not need God.

Psychologism: Always follow feelings.

License: Freedom is, "Do what you want to do".

Hedonism: Joy and pleasure are the same.

Individualism: I want mine!

Children need to learn how to substitute true Christian ideals for these false ideals:

Truth is what is real.

"Without Me you can do nothing" (Jn 15:5).

Do what you know is right.

True freedom is, "Do what is right".

True joy is self-giving.

"Love your neighbor as yourself" (Mt 19:19).

Our Core Group reflected on how difficult it is for children to understand religion, unless adults help them understand the difference between worldly values and the message of Jesus.[7] We cannot isolate children from worldly influences, but we must somehow teach them how to discern and judge.

In the course of our deliberations, we recalled how Arius, the fourth century heretic, was enormously successful in spreading his false ideas through the medium of popular songs. Perhaps songs will work for us too. We decided to try.

---

[7] We came to this insight and decided to do something about it, by learning of the experience of Alphonse Nabreda, SJ in Japan. Father Nabreda found that he had to address certain aspects of Japanese culture before his students could even understand what he was trying to teach them. It is our opinion that we too live in a culture that contains elements just as inimical to the understanding of the Christian message.

During the next several months we developed six songs[8] to illustrate the Slimy Principles.

THE LITTLE DOGGIE
(Subjectivism)

There was a little doggie, sitting on a porch.
For you he was a doggie; for me he was a horse.
"Beg pardon," said the old baboon, swinging into sight.
"I do declare, I do declare, that *both* of you are right."
"I'm sorry," said the wise old owl, who just then came
  along.
"I do declare, I do declare, that *one* of you is wrong
"I do declare a doggie's there, not horse or cow or
  mink.
"A thing is always what it is, in spite of what you
  think.
"A thing is always what it is, in spite of what you
  think.
"A dog's a dog, a cow's a cow, and neither one's a
  mink."

THE BRAWNY LAD
(Pelagianism)

Once there was a brawny lad,
Who thought he knew it all.
Too bad, the thing he didn't know:
That pride precedes a fall.
He thought he owned his very self,
Apart from God who made him
A brawny lad can do all right,
Without the Lord to save him.

---

[8] The musical accompaniment for the six songs is in *Appendix C.*

So all through life he never knew
How God's love held him fast,
Until one day, God's hand removed,
He landed on his ...

THE 'GATOR
(Psychologism)
When a person follows feelings,
Instead of what he knows,
It's a thought a big ol' 'gator
Has him firmly by the nose.
Pull him this way, pull him that way,
Pull him all around.
Since he doesn't follow reason,
Won't he end up upside down?

THE DO-DO BIRD
(License)
"I am free," said the Do-Do Bird,
"Free to be bad, if I like;
"To razzle and dazzle, to frizzle and frazzle,
"No matter if wrong or if right.
No wonder you're such a Do-Do Bird;
Not to know what is good in God's sight.
 False freedom is "Do what you want to do"
True freedom is "Do what is right".

DEAR WORLD
(Hedonism)
Dear world, I want to be happy.
Give me money and pleasure and fame.
I want it, I want it, I want it,
Without any suffering or pain.
True joy is the joy of self-giving,
Whatever the world may say.
No money or pleasure can give it;
No sorrow can take it away.

I WANT MINE
(Individualism)
"I want mine," said the Warthog;
"I want mine," said the Toad.
"You can push the rest away, for all I care,
"And send them on down the road."

What can you do, Mr. Warthog?
What can you do, Mr. Toad?
With all the other people being sent on down,
Who is left to help you lighten your load?

Live a little lighter, Mr. Warthog.
Live a little lighter, Mr. Toad.
Think a little more about the rest of us,
Helping you and one another down the road.

We asked our music teacher to teach the songs to the whole school, and he did. In the meantime, our parish[9] hired a teacher of *Wraparound Religion.* We called it wraparound, because its goal is to surround the regular teaching of religion with an understanding of the culture that wraps around everything the children experience in the modern world. The purpose of the program was to help children recognize the slimy principles inherent in radio, television, and movies, and to begin to think in Christian terms.

As we got into the program, we discovered that the upper grades were capable of understanding and applying the concepts; the lower grades were content for the moment with singing the songs.

Our *Wraparound Religion* teacher is very enthusiastic, and is well versed in the philosophical concepts involved. He is testing various pedagogical approaches and hopes eventually to compose a teachers' manual. He also offers mini-courses on the Slimy Principles to parents.

Our *Wraparound Program* is a very small inroad into an overwhelming wilderness of modern errors. We were determined, however, at least to do something. We leave the rest in God's hands.

---

[9]   This teacher was hired by the parish, because he was assigned to provide *Wraparound Religion* not only in our school but in our parish CCD Program.

15.

A Missionary Approach to Renewal
Evangelizing Our School's Culture

FROM THE BEGINNING of the renewal project, our Core Group realized that what we were trying to do came within the definition of "evangelization". According to Pope Paul VI, evangelization means "bringing the Good News into all the strata of humanity, and through its influence, transforming humanity from within and making it new".[1] We wanted to do that in our school--bring Christian ideals into the school's very heart, transforming the school from within.

Evangelization has two dimensions--personal and cultural. Each depends on the other,[2] and each has traditionally been a constitutive element of the missionary activity of the Church. Since we were taking a missionary approach to renewal, we resolved to give attention not only to the personal dimension, but to the cultural as well.[3]

---

[1]   Paul VI, *On Evangelization in the Modern World, Apostolic Exhortation Evangelii Nuntiandi, December 8, 1975*, n. 18.

[2]   *Ibid.*, nn. 19-20.

As we use the term here, culture is "a system of shared expectations about how things ought to be". The expectations may be shared among the inhabitants of an entire nation, or among the members of a subculture such as our school. As a group within a larger whole, our school shares many expectations with other Americans--for example, the right to freedom. Some of our expectations, however, are different--for example, our belief in eternal life. To the extent that our expectations differ from the culture as a whole, we are counter-cultural.

People do not necessarily live up to the expectations of their culture. Even those who believe in stop signs, may occasionally fail to stop. Of course, if a plurality of people start running stop signs, the expectation, and thus the culture itself, is likely to change. There are countries where such a thing has happened; stop signs exist, but nobody pays attention to them. At any given time, however, shared expectations, rather than behavior, define the culture.

Expectations are first of all in the mind, even though expectations generally find outward expression. The school's statement of purpose in the *Handbook* is an outward expression; so is the wearing of the school uniform. Outward expressions may take various forms--words, good example, stories, discussions, object lessons, art, music, symbols, and the like.

When we looked at the culture of our school we found very little unity of mind. Students, teachers and parents brought expectations that had seeped into their consciousness from the culture at large. Very few agreed on what the school was supposed to do, or on how it should do it. The resulting hostility, hurt feelings, and unhappiness brought our school to the edge of the dysfunctional. This lack of shared expectations did not make for a healthy school culture.

---

[3]   In reflecting on the missionary approach to culture, we were instructed by the work of Louis J. Luzbetak, *The Church and Cultures: New Perspectives in Missiological Anthropology* (Orbis, 1988). We were profoundly inspired by the renewal at Franciscan University of Steubenville. See: Michael Scanlan, *Let the Fire Fall* (Franciscan University Press, 1997). We were helped in our thinking by Timothy J. Cook, *Architects of Catholic Culture: Designing & Building Catholic Culture in Catholic Schools* (NCEA, 2001).

We saw our task, therefore, as one of clarifying the expectations; aligning expectations with the Gospel and local circumstances; and creating unity around those expectations. In this way, we proposed to evangelize our school's culture.

From the beginning of the project, our Core Group realized that as our purpose, goals and approaches came into sharper focus, there would be danger that parents whose ideas were not in alignment would tend to withdraw their children from our school. We were prepared to take that risk. We did not want to survive as an institution at the price of watering down our Catholic identity. Fortunately, the school did survive the shock of culture change, the withdrawals were minimal, and the enrollment even increased. We hope this increase resulted from parents' perception that our school offered something special and desirable, even though we were not able (or inclined) to compete with the public school in facilities or scope of programs.

Chapters 4 through 14 tell the story of how we clarified the expectations and aligned the expectations with the Gospel. In the present chapter we relate how we tried to bring the expectations into unity, in a deliberate effort to induce cultural change.

There are two engines of cultural change: knowledge and behavior. What people *know* about cigarette smoking can influence their expectations about the dangers of smoking. People might learn about the dangers of smoking through advertising campaigns, warnings on cigarette packages, advice of their doctors, the testimony of movie stars, school programs, the advice of friends, experiencing the death of a loved one caused by smoking, and the like.

Changing *behavior* can also change attitudes and expectations (Aristotle). There can be laws against selling cigarettes to minors; there can be multi-million dollar lawsuits; and there can be prohibitions against smoking in public places. People may not like these restrictions, but after years of acting *as though* smoking is wrong, people begin to develop an attitude that smoking *is* wrong.

As these expectations become common to more and more people, society reaches a point where smoking is generally thought to be bad. Such public opinion does not mean that no one smokes. The change in public opinion means only that the culture has changed.

Changing the culture within a small organization like our school employs the same engines of change: knowledge and behavior. But we add a third--grace. God's grace can change people's attitudes and expectations, and draw individuals together into a sense of unity that is the hallmark of every effective group. Prayer accompanied every stage of our renewal process. The other things we did are described below.

Knowledge

In the initial small group meetings with parents and teachers, we explained our basic philosophy: *Statement of Principles.*[4] We involved the participants in discussing issues and policies, both during the meetings and informally throughout the process. We invited those willing to read books and devote time to working for renewal to join the Core Group. Bulletins, homilies, and informal networks provided ongoing communication. We decided not to hold general meetings, preferring to work in less cumbersome small groups.

When we drafted the *Handbook*, we called for comments before finalization. There was virtually no response, but parents, teachers, and parishioners had ample opportunity to study detailed descriptions of the school's philosophy, purpose, and policies. To encourage study, we asked parents to give us written assurance that the materials in the *Handbook* were acceptable to them.

At this time, we began to offer parents of new students a four-hour orientation, covering the material in the *Handbook*, and stressing what we called the five pillars: basics in teaching, repentance in discipline, parental involvement, Christian motivation for study, and God's grace. Before being allowed to

---

[4] *Appendix D.*

register their child, parents were asked to sign a *Memorandum of Agreement.*[5]   The practice of holding such an extensive orientation for new parents has contributed much toward creating unity of expectations. In seven more years, all parents will have received this orientation.

Behavior

We decided to introduce all behavioral changes at once, instead of gradually. Thus we employed the revolutionary rather than the gradual approach to cultural change.[6] One reason was that culture shock would call attention to just how different we were expecting our school to be.

Grammar Games helped teachers understand what we meant by "remembering" as a teaching goal.   Red Codes demonstrated that we would no longer tolerate disruption in class.   Changes in the By-Laws of the Home and School Association clarified that organization's spiritual goals, and placed fund-raising under school governance.   Publication of Iowa Test results in leaflet form gave assurance to parents and parishioners that students were achieving to capacity.

Re-orienting discipline into repentance placed this element of school life into a more spiritual context. Involving students in writing the *Book of Chivalry* had a marked effect on school courtesy.   Requiring more student effort in the study of religion emphasized school priorities.   Outlawing behaviorism in our school moved teachers to use motivational systems that were more spiritual. Requiring certain grades to attend Forty Hours instead of Trick-or-Treat gave parents and children an opportunity to choose right priorities. Expecting Sunday Mass attendance demonstrated our school's seriousness about religion, and released the flow of grace.

Dealing with crises in accordance with the *Handbook* exemplified the meaning of the principles the *Handbook*

---

[5] See page 89.

[6] Luzbetak, *The Church and Cultures*, pp. 295-296.

contained. Eliminating frivolous complaints freed our principal to spend time assisting teachers in class.

We were able to make these radical changes in behavior because we were part of a hierarchical Church, with real authority to set policy, even in opposition to the popular will. In exercising authority, however, we tried our best to offer *leadership*. We had recourse to philosophical-theological principles, we took seriously the truly horrible values (as well as the good values) the world offered to our children, we listened carefully to parents, and we prayed as hard as we could.

Finally, we gave attention to language, which, anthropologists tell us, is a prominent element in cultural change. All important social institutions have their own special language. For example, baseball players use the word "bunt", musicians use "atonal", politicians use "filibuster", brokers use "bull market", programmers use "megabytes", physicists use "relativity". Words like these, whether in common usage or not, not only provide means of communication within institutions, but also contribute to an inward sense of solidarity as well as to an outward sense of respect. For this reason, we have made a special point of using church words within our school--liturgical quadrangle, beadle, vespers, Kohathites, *eutraphalia*, aspergil, Tenebrae, provost, Forty Hours, trolygytes, Mardi Gras, acolyte, credence table, Pelagianism, and the like. We would not want our children to think that the Church is the only institution so unimportant that she has no special language of her own.

Cultural change is a complex process. Multiple approaches are necessary; there is no simple formula. The changes we made were so numerous and substantial, and so rapid, that a climate of tension ensued, affecting even those who accepted the changes and welcomed the new approach. Prayer was our recourse. Nevertheless, it took about a year for the tension to subside.

We now hope that parents, teachers, and students will be able to come closer to one another in real affection. Already teachers report that it is easier to be affectionate toward students, because students themselves are behaving better and showing greater courtesy. Certainly the elimination of venting by angry parents has created a new willingness on the part of teachers to take parents into their confidence. For our part, the consolidation of expectations that has occurred so far has made the members of the Core Group less fearful that any group of parents will want to challenge our central principles. At this point, affection urges us to invite the parents into closer collaboration with the life, work, and policy-making of the school.

The preceding chapters have explained the process our Core Group undertook. It is now time to look at what teachers, parents and eighth graders think about the changes that we have made.

16.

What Parents, Teachers, And Students Say
Our Strengths and Weaknesses

Our SPRING SURVEY asks parents, teachers and eighth grade students to tell us what they believe to be the strengths and weaknesses of our school. In addition, we ask parents to state, in order of priority, the reasons why they send their children to our school. The survey is confidential, and names are not signed. The results reported here are after the second year of the renewal program.

Parent Survey

Forty-one of our 141 parents completed the survey, a response rate of 34 percent. Seventy-one percent of those who responded said they *sent their children to our school* primarily for religious reasons (religious teaching and environment); twenty-six percent primarily for academic reasons (especially grammar and math); and three percent primarily for safety reasons. Other considerations included: good teachers, personal attention to children (small classes), teaching of manners and respect, discipline, good companions, less expensive than other private schools, family tradition, close to home, volunteer program for children, dress code, full-day kindergarten, respect for minorities, and safe environment.

The following *weaknesses* were indicated; the number in parentheses indicates the number of parents: school building needs to be improved (3); hot lunch should be more than once a week (7); dreary building atmosphere (1); failure to follow through on discipline policies (9); priest not in classroom frequently enough (1); Catholic students making non-Catholic children feel defensive (1); not enough males on faculty (1); computer program (5); failure to provide bus service (1); not enough communication between teachers and students (1); some classes too large (1); too much homework at times (1); absence of academic fair (1); not enough activities at recess (1); not enough extracurricular activities (1); one unkind staff person (2); not enough space (1); science curriculum (1); library program (1); lack of special events to promote school spirit (2); relying on small children to bring notes to parents (1); memorizing *Catholic Definitions* (2); math program (1); elimination of former programs (1); no high school algebra course (1); memorizing poems as penance (1).

Parents listed the following as school *strengths*: small size of school allows individual attention (9); good discipline (10); encouragement of reading (2); grammar emphasis (5); mathematics program (5); no fluff school projects (1); consistent policies (1); good communication with parents (2); loving, respectful Christian atmosphere (14); decisions based on what is best for children, not what other schools do (1); good teachers and staff (17); extracurricular activities (1); religious program (21); good academics, especially basics (6); interaction among Grades K-8 (1); unifying philosophy (1); sensitivity to financial needs of parents (1); children truly taught by example (1); emphasis on teaching morals (1); school part of good parish (1); dress code (1).

Eighth Grade Survey

Regarding *academics*, the students expressed overwhelming support for the math program, grammar program, religion program (including *Wraparound Religion*), and social science. They identified the science and computer programs as weaknesses. Regarding *school setting*, the students listed as strengths the teachers, the manners program, Mass and prayer in the school, the Ministry of Repentance, and the presence of seminarians. They listed as weaknesses having hot lunch only once a week, not enough library books, and not enough recess equipment.

Teacher Survey

Here is what the teachers have to say, in their own words: "What are the strengths? I have been pleased with the new system. I am very pleased with the results of the Grammar Games. Each year the children remember more, and you can really see the step-by-step building process. We have heard many good comments. The *Chivalry* books are used each year. We have been picking out different things to work on with the children, and I have noticed more children responding. The *Catholic Definitions* continue to be a success. The children have done such a great job learning them."

"What are the strengths? School comes before all the fun stuff. Grammar is excellent. Children are expected to attend Sunday Mass. There are not a lot of fund-raisers. What are the weaknesses? Parish sports program. We do not represent ourselves well. We are not following the *Handbook* on discipline policy. We are allowing students into school who have been in trouble. Parents are telling us how the school should be run. We need to be stronger in standing firm with our belief that the school is there for the students' education. Religion and academics are the priority. We should also encourage our students to be mannerly always, and wear appropriate clothing at school, at sports, and at church. Teachers should have more say in what needs improvement. We see the concerns; we know the problem areas. The *Handbook* should be followed consistently."

"What are the strengths? Discipline, staff, benefits, principal's leadership, and the respect received from students. What are the weaknesses? Students' writing ability; need to update uniforms and add summer uniform. What improvements are needed? School building needs attention, especially bathroom situation and dampness in basement classrooms. The upper grades need to go back to the vocabulary-based spelling series, to prepare them for high school."

"What are the strengths? Grammar; stability that has come from the five pillars explained to parents at orientation: basics, discipline, parental involvement, Christian motivation for study, and grace. What are the weaknesses? The computer program."

"What are the strengths? The Repentance Ministry holds students responsible for the moral decisions they make. It provides for spiritual healing and strengthens powers of memory and concentration. It allows the Minister of Repentance to counsel each student and have a meaningful dialog. Some teachers do not take advantage of this program, because of the inconvenience of filling out the form. This laxity can lead to problems later on. Only good things have come out of the *Wraparound Religion* program. It makes the students conscious of the evil in the world, and it reinforces the morals of our Catholic Faith. The grammar program builds the basic knowledge of the English language, and helps them prepare for high school. Their knowledge of grammar helps them become more successful in other areas of the curriculum. The *Student Prayer* provides a constant reminder of why they are here, and how God's grace is important for their success. The *Book of Chivalry* helps us teach students that manners are very important in life."

"What are the strengths? Grammar, *Catholic Definitions*, *Wraparound Religion*, faculty, staff and administration, Friday Mass and other spiritual exercises. What are the weaknesses? Lack of playground equipment, lack of computers in class, not enough parental involvement during lunch and recess."

"What are the strengths? The *Wraparound Religion* program exposes our children to how they should be living, and not how society accepts certain morals today. The principal takes the teacher's word over the child's perception of how things happened. One of my favorite reasons for working here is that our principal has always backed me up and supported me. Grammar, grammar, grammar! Need I say more? What would I like to see improved? More involvement of families, such as Grandparents' Day, Career Day, etc. Although I agree with our policy that does not reward children for what they should be doing, I do think we could give them occasional surprises (special snack, dress down day, school color day, etc.). We all love to receive a break sometimes, and we are dealing with children five to fourteen. Our principal continues to hear positive comments from high school teachers concerning the grammar. I am proud to be a part of such a well-respected place of learning!"

"What are the strengths? There are many. We have worked hard to teach and live our *Statement of Principles*. This effort was evident in the behavior and attitudes of parents and students this school year. We also have a strong foundation of the five pillars in our school. We have a strong religion program with *Wraparound Religion* and *Catholic Definitions*. The Grammar Games and grammar studies have made large differences in our students. What are the weaknesses? Our computer program."

What happens to these concerns and suggestions? We take them seriously, and intend to do our best to give them respectful consideration, even when we do not entirely agree. Some of the ideas are in the administrative category, such as providing more library books and recess equipment, reviewing the science program, and monitoring the implementation of the *Handbook*.

Other issues are questions of policy, which the School Committee intends to study in detail. We are studying the potential use of computers for instructional purposes. We need to do more work in consolidating parental consensus about the nature and purpose of our school. We have made progress, but we need to do much more. We need to present our school more effectively to the community at large, through the Grammar Bee, a possible Academic Fair, and other means. Finally, we need to draw parents more closely into the heart of the school, without sacrificing teacher authority, or endangering our newly-established principles. There is no shortage of things to be done.

17.

Catholic from the Inside Out?
Not Yet.   We Need Help.

I N THE PAST FEW YEARS we have tried to give glory to
God by helping parents educate their children. Recognizing that
the children entrusted to our care are created in God's image, we
have defined our goal as helping them live up to that image by
becoming good citizens of this life and the next. We have tried
to give glory to God by teaching children what they need to learn
at the elementary level (our direct goal); and by providing a
setting six and one-half hours a day where children may receive
love, inspiration and good example, and in turn may respond by
giving something of themselves to others and to God (our
indirect goal). We have called our children to repentance when
they have done wrong. We have tried to make them understand
that not just religion class, but that all their studies, and all their
good deeds are important for building the Kingdom of God. We
have tried to make our students aware of the glorious message of
Jesus, and of the dangers that lurk in today's culture. We have
tried to challenge our children to develop all their talents, to
study hard for love of God, and to find joy in their life and work,
even when confronted with the cross. We have tried to permeate
the atmosphere of our school with a sense of humble trust in

God's grace. And we have tried to create a quality, bare-bones school that the Catholics in our area, who are of modest income, can afford.

We believe that with God's help, we have made some progress on all these fronts. But we have not yet crossed the line beyond which our school can be said to be truly Catholic from the inside out.

Why not? We have much more to do ourselves. But in addition, at this point we cannot cross the line *without outside help.*

We do have some degree of outside help already. There are Catholic leadership programs for principals.[1] Our principal has attended one of them, and currently conducts a mentoring program within our school. Week-long retreats are available, although we devoutly hope that someone will soon develop a nationwide network of retreats specifically for teachers. Teachers do have opportunities for studying pedagogy, child development, and the subject matter they are teaching, through programs offered by local colleges and by our diocese. All of this is helpful; but we have three additional needs that cannot be met without outside help.[2]

1. Books

The first need is for *books that connect teachers to the Catholic educational tradition.* Since the second century, the Church has been involved in formal education. Think of Origen and the second century school at Alexandria; the monastic schools such as Fulda, Iona and Monte Cassino; the cathedral and parish schools of the early middle ages; Boethius,

---

[1]   Seton Hall, Notre Dame, Catholic University, NCEA St Mary's University the Diocese of Arlington , the Diocese of Providence and others conduct such programs. Maria Ciriello, ed., *Formation and Development for Catholic School Leaders* (USCC, 1994).

[2]   "Teachers have a right to expect...training.... Specialized teacher training centers should be established to give the kind of professional training that will help Catholic educators to fulfill their mission." Edwin J. McDermott, *Distinctive Qualities of the Catholic School* (NCEA, 1997), p. 46.

Cassiodorus, Isidore of Seville, Venerable Bede, Alcuin at the court of Charlemagne; Rabanus Maurus, Bruno, Odo of Cluny, Abelard, Peter Lombard, Albert the Great, Thomas Aquinas, Bonaventure; the great universities that evolved from the cathedral schools: Paris, Bologna, Salamanca, Coimbra, Oxford, Cambridge, Padua;   Hugh of St. Victor and his educational philosophy, Didascalicon; the worldwide Jesuit educational system of the Renaissance; Newman, Doupanloup; de La Salle and the Brothers of the Christian Schools; Don Bosco, Mother Seton; the Oratory, Vincentians, Sulpicians; the many orders of Sisters: Notre Dame, Visitation, Sisters of Charity, Sisters of St. Joseph, Sisters of Mercy, School Sisters of Notre Dame, Ursulines, Loretto, Nazareth, Dominicans, Sacred Heart, Immaculate Heart of Mary, Blessed Sacrament.

After all these centuries, there is much wisdom to be mined. Our teachers need to come into contact with this wisdom, and to become familiar with the educational approaches of founders, Saints, and outstanding Catholic teachers.[3]

Our teachers also need *books to deepen their understanding of the Catholic philosophical-theological approach to elementary education.* In the course of our project, we consulted a number of these books.[4] Valuable as these older books are and continue to be, philosophical-theological writing needs to be ongoing. Issues and challenges continually arise. An example

---

3   Examples of the types of works we mean: Timothy Walch, *Parish School: American Catholic Parochial Education from Colonial Times to the Present* (Crossroad, 1996); Edward A. Fitzpatrick, *LaSalle;*   John Morrison, *The Educational Philosophy of St. John Bosco* (Salesiana Publishers, 1979); Buetow, *Of Singular Benefit;*   Curtis, *Educating the Faithful: Religion;* George A. Van Grieken, *Touching the Hearts of Students: Characteristics of a LaSallian School* (De LaSalle Institute, 1999); Christopher J. Kauffman, *Education and Transformation: Marianist Ministries in America since 1849* (Crossroad, 1999). We would like to know more about Vittorino daFeltre (1378-1446), who in his school named "The House of Joy", imparted to the unruly Gonzaga children such high ideals that it became the wonder of Renaissance Italy. DaFeltre is mentioned by McGucken, *Catholic Way*, p. 125. (There are of course, numerous lives of founders and saints; these are inspiring, but contain few specifics about their educational philosophy and methods.) In looking for materials, we found a valuable source: Hunt, *Research in Catholic Education.*

[4]   See *Catholic Books We Consulted.Appendix*

would be the task of clarifying the goals and purposes of the new types of Catholic schools that are emerging today.

2. Critiques of Educational Methods

Our teachers need Catholic *critiques of past and present teaching methods that originate in the secular schools of education.* No doubt such methods contain much of value; but secular methods need to be assessed and baptized.[5] Secular methods sometimes have philosophical roots in relativism, subjectivism, positivism, naturalism, or behaviorism.[6] Unless Catholic scholars provide theological-philosophical critiques, our teachers are at the mercy of the latest fad.[7] Offering critiques of educational methods is beyond the level of competence of our Core Group; professional help is needed. We are firmly convinced that our school cannot become fully Catholic until the methods forming the basis of our teaching have been evaluated and firmly rooted in Catholic assumptions and sensibilities.[8]

---

[5] Examples of critiques: C. Heltsley, "Opening the Classroom Door to a Stranger and Leaving the Room: The Importance of Scrutinizing Values Implanted in Computer Software", *Momentum, 29:4, 53-61;* Ronald J. Nuzzi, "Cooperative Learning and Catholic Schools", *Momentum, 29:1, 70-75;* Redden and Ryan discuss the relationship of philosophy to method extensively in John D. Redden and Francis A. Ryan, *A Catholic Philosophy of Education* (Bruce, 1956), pp. 276-323.

[6] "Teachers in Catholic schools should examine the methods they use as individuals, and the methods of the school as a whole, to determine if the methods enhance, allow, or inhibit gospel living. Each method should be examined from the perspective of faith, from the viewpoint of quality education, and with the good of each student in mind. Only if methods meet the above criteria should they be implemented." Mary Leanne Welch, *Methods of Teaching in the Catholic School* (NCEA, 1987), p. 79.

[7] As early as 1917, Shields offered a caution on this point. Shields, *Philosophy of Education, p. 7.*

[8] Fortunately, Catholic educators offer a number of new and creative teaching methods that take Catholic principles as their starting point. This is especially true for religious education. Catherine Dooley, "The Religious Education Curriculum in Catholic Schools", in Youniss, *Catholic Character of Catholic Schools.* Thomas Lickona, *Educating for Character: How Our Schools Can Teach Respect and Responsibility* (Bantam, 1991). Patricia H. Cronin, *Character Development in the Catholic School* (NCEA, 1999).

3. Courses and Summer Workshop

Our teachers need courses and workshops on *fundamentals of Catholic schooling*. We want them to know the Catholic teaching about truth and moral goodness, the nature and destiny of human beings, and how people acquire knowledge. Teachers need to know that there are different types of Catholic schools, each with specific goals. They need to be exposed to Catholic critiques of secular educational methods. Our teachers need to learn the history of Catholic schooling, and who the key figures are in our educational tradition.[9]

It would be unfortunate, even tragic, if teacher-training programs which do not fully integrate the concepts of objective truth, morality, the afterlife, redemption, original sin, and grace into the heart of their instruction on educational purposes and methods, should be allowed the last word in the professional preparation of teachers for Catholic schools.

In testimony to our own needs, we hereby add our voice to those who are calling for more support for lay teachers in Catholic schools. Timothy Cook, of Creighton University, puts

---

[9] In September of 2002, we mailed surveys to the 163 Catholic institutions identified by the Association of Catholic Colleges and Universities as having teacher training programs. The institutions were asked if they offered courses, workshops, or seminars on the philosophy, theology, or history of Catholic education, suitable for laity who are teaching, or preparing to teach, in Catholic elementary schools. We received 115 responses. The 46 colleges and universities who said they had such offerings are listed here. Some institutions offer summer workshops, some offer courses during the school year, and some offer both. CA: Loyola Marymount University; Santa Clara University. HI: Chaminade University. IA: Briar Cliff University; Clarke College; Loras College; Mount Mercy College. IL: Dominican University. IN: Calumet College of Saint Joseph; Marian College; Saint Joseph's College. KS: Newman University. LA: Our Lady of Holy Cross College; Xavier University of Louisiana. MI: Madonna University. MN: The College of St. Catherine. MO: Rockhurst University. MT: University of Great Falls. NE: Creighton University. NJ: Felician College; Georgian Court College; Seton Hall University. NY: Manhattan College; Niagara University. OH: College of Mount Saint Joseph; Franciscan University of Steubenville; Notre Dame College of Ohio; Ohio Dominican University; University of Dayton; Xavier University. OR: University of Portland. PA: Alvernia College; Chestnut Hill College; Gannon University; Gwynedd-Mercy College; Holy Family College; Seton Hill University; University of Scranton. TN: Aquinas College; Christian Brothers University. TX: St. Edward's University; University of St. Thomas. VA: Marymount University. WA: St. Martin's College. WI: Alverno College; Mount Mary College, Silver Lake College; Viterbo University.

it well: "It is incumbent upon teacher education programs at Catholic colleges and universities to intentionally and systematically foster an appreciation of teaching as a vocation and nurture teacher candidates in their personal spirituality and public ministry.... All involved in Catholic education must investigate new models for building communities of faith and learning among teachers today."[10]

Who knows what form support for Catholic teachers needs to take? One thing is clear, however. The need is there, and the need is urgent.

~ ~ ~

It is our prayer that with the help of God, and the assistance of the wider Church, our school will be able to give more and more glory to God, and some day actually cross over into the happy category of being Catholic from the inside out.

In the meantime, what inspires us is a vision of spiritual regeneration in which we hope our school will be able to play a humble part:

> [The Catholic Faith] ... has entered into human
> history and changed its course. It shows how a
> seed of new life was implanted in humanity by the
> setting apart of a particular people as the channel
> of revelation which found its fulfillment in the
> Incarnation of the Divine Word in a particular person
> at a particular moment of history. It shows how this
> new life was communicated to a spiritual society which

---

[10]   Timothy Cook, *Catholic Education: A Journal of Inquiry and Practice*, 5:2, 259-260. As this book was going to press, we became aware of the excellent study by John Watzke of Notre Dame, "Teacher Education Practices in Catholic Higher Education", *Catholic Education*, 6:2, 138-167. Watzke documents the issues facing Catholic schools as they turn to Catholic Colleges for help in Catholic teacher training.

became the organ of the divine action in history, so
that the human race may be progressively spiritualized
and raised to a higher spiritual plane.[11]

What has happened in just a few years in our lowly school, which has very few computers and not even a hot lunch program, convinces us without a shadow of a doubt that we can be part of this glorious process, and that God will help us to do so, because His grace is everywhere.

---

[11]   Christopher Dawson, *The Crisis of Western Education* (Sheed & Ward, 1961), p. 201.

Our Book of Chivalry

How to Be Courteous, Gallant,
Generous and Magnanimous

1. CHIVALRY IN CLASS

Courteous:
1. Pay attention when your teacher or another student is speaking in class. (Don't daydream.)

Gallant:
2. Gentlemen remove hats before entering a building.
3. Carry tissue or a handkerchief, to send your germs into when you cough or sneeze.
4. Hold doors for teachers and others. (Don't let doors slam in their face.)
5. Offer to help carry heavy things for teachers.

Generous:
6. Lend your things to others, when they ask.

Respectful:
7. Dress neatly.
8. Raise your hand before speaking. (Don't blurt out.)
9. Answer properly. (Don't use 'yeah' or 'nope.')

Magnanimous:
10. Do kind things for others, even those you do not like.

~ ~ ~

"Listen to counsel and receive instruction, that you may eventually become wise. (Proverbs 19:20)"

Get help from the saint who helped to give us Catholic schools. "St. Elizabeth Seton, pray for us!"

2. CHIVALRY ON THE PLAYGROUND

Courteous:
1. Expand your vocabulary of exclamations! There are plenty of good ones around.

Gallant:
2. Think of the feelings of others when choosing up teams.

Respectful:
3. Treat every person as you would treat Jesus Christ. See Christ in everyone.

Magnanimous:
4. In choosing players for your team, sometimes pick people who aren't so good, or whom you don't especially like.

~ ~ ~

"Love your neighbor as yourself" (Mk 12:31).

Get help from the saint who specialized in playgrounds. "Saint John Bosco, pray for us!"

3. CHIVALRY TOWARD GROWN-UPS

Courteous:
1. Say "please, thank you, you're welcome."
2. Grown-ups have names. Use them when speaking to

them. Example, "Good morning, Miss Jones."

3. Answer the phone in the way your parents tell you. Give out only the information they want you to give. But be courteous to callers. Say, "May I tell them who's calling?" (Not, "Who is it?"). Use correct grammar. Say, "This is he." (Not, "This is him).

Respectful:

4. Speak to grown-ups when you meet them in school. (Don't just walk by.)

5. When you speak to grown-ups, look them in the eye.

~ ~ ~

"When among your elders, be not forward" (Sir 32:9).

Get help from the patron saint of courtesy. St. Francis de Sales, pray for us!

4. CHIVALRY IN SPORTS

Courteous:

1. Be a good sport. (Don't be a sore loser. Winning isn't everything.)

2. Have confidence in your skill and training, but do not boast.

Gallant:

3. Try to win, but not at any cost. (Never cheat to win.)

4. Be kind to your team mates when they make a mistake.

Respectful:

5. See Christ in the players on the other team. Treat them with respect.

6. Respect the decision of the referee, even when you think he is wrong.

7. Be kind to your coach. Be thankful for all your coach does for you!

Magnanimous:
    8. Do your best, and offer the game up to God.

"I have fought the good fight, I have finished the race, I have kept the Faith" (2 Ti 4:7).

Get help from the Apostle who loved sports. "St. Paul, pray for us!"

5. CHIVALRY IN CHURCH

Courteous:
    1. Give God your undivided attention in Church. (Don't do anything to distract others.)
    2. Stay in church at least till the end of the "thank you" hymn at the end.

Gallant:
    3. Carry out your assigned duties with reverence: bringing the gifts, lector, server.
    4. At the Kiss of Peace, show reverence and respect for Jesus in your neighbor. (Not a time for chit-chat.)

Generous:
    5. At the Consecration of the Mass, offer all the sacrifices you make in school, and in the rest of your life, to God through Jesus, who offered Himself on the cross.
    6. At hymn time, sing out!

Respectful:
    7. Fast from food and drink (except medicine and water) one hour before you receive Holy Communion.
    8. Dress appropriately when you come to church.
    9. Genuflect before Our Lord present in the Tabernacle, when you come into or leave church, and every time you pass before the Blessed Sacrament.

~ ~ ~

"I will go in to the altar of God, the God who gives joy to my youth" (Ps. 42).

Get help from the saint who prepared the way of the Lord. "St. John the Baptist, pray for us!"

6. CHIVALRY AT TABLE

Courteous:
1. Say Grace before the meal, to ask Our Lord's blessing on the food you are about to eat. Say Grace after the meal, to thank Our Lord for what He has provided.
2. Say "please" and "thank you" when you ask to have food passed to you. (Don't reach out and grab it.}
3. Eat politely. (Don't slurp! Don't be a *rudis*.)

Gallant:
4. Be sure to thank the person who prepared the meal.

Respectful:
5. Take your time in eating, and join politely in the table conversation.
6. A meal is a social event; stay to the end. If there is a very good reason to leave before the end, politely ask to be excused, and say Grace.

Magnanimous:
7. When there's not enough of what you like to go around, give the best things to your brothers and sisters.

~ ~ ~

"Whether you eat or drink - whatever you do - you should do all for the glory of God" (1 Cor 10:31).

Get help from the saint who gave food to the poor. "St. Vincent de Paul, pray for us."

Some Catholic Definitions
That Children May Learn by Heart

WHY LEARN BY HEART?

Our Holy Father, Pope John Paul II, has this to say:

"We are all aware that this method [memorization] can present certain disadvantages, not the least of which is that it lends itself to insufficient ... assimilation, reducing all knowledge to formulas that are repeated without being properly understood. These disadvantages ... have in some places led to the almost complete suppression--according to some, alas, the definitive suppression--of memorization in catechesis.... The blossoms, if we may call them that, of faith and piety do not grow in the desert places of a memory-less catechesis. What is essential is that the texts that are memorized must at the same time be taken in and gradually understood in depth, in order to become a source of Christian life." (*Catechesi Tradendae*, n. 55.)

The *National Catechetical Directory* states in paragraph 176:

"While catechesis cannot be limited to the repetition of formulas and it is essential that formulas and facts pertaining to faith be understood, memorization has nevertheless had a special place in the handing-on of the faith throughout the ages and should continue to have such a place today."

The purpose of this pamphlet is to provide a handy compendium of fifty-four Catholic definitions, which may be memorized over a nine-year period from kindergarten to eighth grade. The wording of the definitions has been adapted from the *Catechism of the Catholic Church,* to which reference is given in the text.

This pamphlet is neither a catechism, nor a catechetical text-book, since it does not contain everything that children should learn about religion during their elementary school years. Neither does it contain all possible Catholic definitions, but only those the author has selected as useful for children of that age. I hope that having these fifty-four definitions all together in one place will provide an aid to many who give themselves so generously to the task of handing on the Faith.

KINDERGARTEN

1. **Sign of the Cross.** In the name of the Father, and of the Son and of the Holy Spirit. Amen.

2. **Angel of God.** Angel of God, my guardian dear, to whom His love entrusts me here; ever this day be at my side, to light and guard, to rule and guide. Amen.

3. **Hail Mary.** Hail Mary, full of grace! The Lord is with thee; blessed art thou among women, and blessed is the Fruit of thy womb, Jesus. Holy Mary, Mother of God, pray for us sinners, now and at the hour of our death. Amen.

4. **Grace before Meals.** Bless us, O Lord, and these Your gifts which we are about to receive from Your bounty, through Christ our Lord. Amen.

FIRST GRADE

5. **Who made us?** God made us from nothing, and keeps us in being from moment to moment by His almighty power. [295-301]

6. **Why did God make us?** God made us to show forth His goodness, and let us share in His own blessed life. [1]

7. **What does God call us to do?** God calls us to seek Him, to know Him, to love Him with all our strength, and to be happy with Him in heaven. [1, 1720-1724]

8. **What do we mean by the Blessed Trinity?** By the Blessed Trinity we mean three Persons in one God. [238-267]

9. **Which are the three persons of the Blessed Trinity?** The three persons of the Blessed Trinity are God the Father, God the Son, and God the Holy Spirit. [62-69]

10. **Lord's Prayer.** Our Father, Who art in heaven, hallowed be Thy name; Thy kingdom come; Thy will be done on earth as it is in heaven. Give us this day our daily bread; and forgive us our trespasses, as we forgive those who trespass against us; and lead us not into temptation, but deliver us from evil. Amen. [2759-2865]

11. **Glory to the Father.** Glory to the Father, and to the Son, and to the Holy Spirit; as it was in the beginning, is now, and will be forever. Amen.

SECOND GRADE

12. **Who is Jesus Christ?** Jesus Christ is the second person of the Holy Trinity, true God and true man. [430-455]

13. **Why did Jesus suffer on the cross?** Jesus suffered on the cross to atone for our sins, and to obtain for us eternal life. [606-623]

14. **Act of Contrition.** My God, I am sorry for all my sins because they displease you, Who are all good and deserving of all my love. With your help I will sin no more. Amen.

15. **How do we share in the cross of Jesus?** We share in the cross of Jesus by joining our sacrifices to the sacrifice of Jesus in the Mass. Participating in the Mass on Sundays and Holy Days is a great privilege and a strict obligation. Those who deliberately fail in this obligation commit a grave sin. [2181]

THIRD GRADE

16. **What is the Church?** The Church is the People of God, the communion of baptized persons who profess the faith and teaching of Jesus Christ, who participate in His Sacraments, in unity with the pastors whom He has appointed. [748-870]

17. **Who founded the Church?** Jesus Christ founded the Church.

18. **Why did Jesus Christ found the Church?** Jesus Christ founded the Church to bring all people to eternal life.

19. **Who are the pastors of the Church?** The pastors of the Church are the pope and the bishops united with him. [871-945]

20. **Who is the pope?** The pope is the successor of St. Peter, the visible head of the Church.

21. **Who are the bishops?** The bishops are the successors of the apostles.

22. **Apostles Creed.** I believe in God, the Father Almighty, Creator of heaven and earth. I believe in Jesus Christ, His only Son, our Lord. He was conceived by the power of the Holy Spirit and born of the Virgin Mary. He suffered under Pontius Pilate, was crucified, died and was buried. He descended to the dead. On the third day He rose again. He ascended into heaven, and is seated at the right hand of the Father. He will come

again to judge the living and the dead. I believe in the Holy Spirit, the holy catholic Church, the communion of saints, the forgiveness of sins, the resurrection of the body, and life everlasting. Amen.

FOURTH GRADE

23. **What is faith?** Faith is the virtue by which we believe in God and believe all that He has revealed to us, as taught by Holy Church. [1842]

24. **What is hope?** Hope is the virtue by which we desire and trust that God will give us eternal life and the graces to merit it. [1843]

25. **What is charity?** Charity is the virtue by which we love God above all things and our neighbor as ourselves for love of God. [1844]

26. **What are the ten commandments?**

1. I, the Lord, am your God: you shall not have strange Gods before me.
2. You shall not take the name of the Lord, your God, in vain.
3. Remember to keep holy the Lord's Day.
4. Honor your father and your mother.
5. You shall not kill.
6. You shall not commit adultery.
7. You shall not steal.
8. You shall not bear false witness against your neighbor.
9. You shall not covet your neighbor's wife.
10. You shall not covet your neighbor's goods. [2052-2082]

27. **What is prayer?** Prayer is lifting the mind and heart to God. [2558-2758]

28. **What is sin?** Sin is an offense against the law of God, by thought, word, deed, or omission. [1846-1853]

29. **What is mortal sin?** Mortal sin involves (1) serious matter, (2) sufficient reflection, and (3) full consent of the will. [1854-1864]

30. **What is venial sin?** Venial sin lacks (1) serious matter, (2) sufficient reflection, or (3) full consent of the will.

31. **Act of contrition.** O my God, I am heartily sorry for having offended You, and I detest all my sins, because of Your just punishments; but most of all because they offend You, my God, who are all good and deserving of all my love. I firmly resolve, with the help of your grace, to sin no more and to avoid the near occasions of sin.

FIFTH GRADE

32. **What are Sacraments?** Sacraments are outward signs, instituted by Christ, to give us grace, to build up the Church, and to give worship to God. [1113-1134]

33. **What is grace?** Grace is God's free gift of His own life, to heal us from sin and make us holy. [1996-1999]

34. **What is sanctifying grace?** Sanctifying grace is an habitual disposition of soul, to live and act in keeping with God's call. [2000]

35. **What is actual grace?** Actual grace is God's intervention in our lives, to enlighten our minds and move our wills to turn to Him and progress in His friendship. [2000]

36. **Name the Sacraments.** Baptism, Confirmation, Holy Eucharist, Penance, Anointing of the Sick, Holy Orders, Matrimony.

37. **What is Baptism?** Baptism is the Sacrament which frees us from sin, incorporates us into the Church, and gives us rebirth as adopted children of God.

38. What is Confirmation? Confirmation is the Sacrament which perfects the grace of Baptism, binds us more closely to the Church, and gives us the special help of the Holy Spirit in spreading and defending the Faith, by word and deed. [1283-1321]

39. What is the Eucharist? In the Holy Eucharist, under the appearances of bread and wine, the Lord Jesus Christ is contained, offered in sacrifice, received, and remembered. [1322-1344]

40. How is Jesus offered in sacrifice in the Eucharist? Jesus Christ, through the ministry of the priest, associates His Church and all her members with His sacrifice of praise and thanksgiving, offered once for all on the cross, and re-presented in every Mass. [1345-1419]

41. What is the Sacrament of Penance? Penance is the Sacrament whereby sins committed after Baptism are forgiven through God's mercy; and sinners are reconciled with the Church which they have wounded by their sins. [1422-1498]

SIXTH GRADE

42. What is perfect contrition? Perfect contrition is sorrow for sins because sin offends God, whom we love above all things for His own sake. [1452]

43. What is imperfect contrition? Imperfect contrition is sorrow for sins because they are hateful in themselves or because we fear God's punishment. [1453]

SEVENTH GRADE

44. What is the Anointing of the Sick? The Anointing of the Sick gives spiritual and sometimes bodily strength to those in danger of death through illness or old age. [1499-1532]

45. What is Holy Orders? Holy Orders is a Sacrament through which bishops, priests and deacons receive the power to carry out the work that Christ entrusted to the apostles until the end of time. [1536-1600]

46. What is Matrimony? Matrimony is a Sacrament by which a baptized man and woman bind themselves in an intimate partnership for the whole of life, and obtain the grace to help one another seek holiness, and bring up their children as friends of God. [1601-1666]

EIGHTH GRADE

47. How does the Gospel of Jesus Christ reach us today? Christ commanded the apostles, and their successors the popes and the bishops, with the help of the Holy Spirit, faithfully to preserve, preach and spread the Gospel to all peoples until the end of time.

48. What is the New Testament The New Testament is that part of the teachings of the apostles which was expressed in a special way through writings inspired by God. [80-98]

49. What happens to each of us at death? At death, the time of accepting or rejecting God is at an end, and Jesus Christ will judge us in accordance with our faith and works. [1021]

50. After judgment, what happens to us? After judgment, those in God's good graces enter into the blessedness of heaven, either immediately or after purification. Those who have rejected God through unrepented mortal sin go immediately into hell. [1022]

51. What is heaven? Heaven is the face-to-face enjoyment of God, for all eternity, and the enjoyment of all other good things in Him, without any suffering or evil. [1023-1029]

52. What is hell? Hell is the eternal suffering of the loss of God, who is our happiness; it is fire, together with every other kind of evil, without any good. [1033-1037]

53.**What is purgatory?** Purgatory is the temporary suffering of the lack of the vision of God and of other punishments, which remove the remains of sin, making us worthy of seeing God. [1030-1032]

54. **What is the resurrection of the body?** Our bodies will be refashioned and reunited to our souls, by the power of God on the last day, in order to participate eternally in the reward or punishment which is ours. [998-1019]

Appendix C
Six Slimy Principles
Musical Score

THE LITTLE DOGGIE
(Subjectivism)

There was a lit- tle dog- gie sit- ting on a porch. For you he was a dog- gie; for me he was a horse. "Beg par- don," said the old ba- boon, swing- ing in- to sight. "I do de- clare, I do de- clare, that

147

both of you are right." "I'm sor- ry," said the wise old owl who just then came a- long. "I

do de-clare, I do de- clare, that one of you is wrong. I

do de- clare a dog- gie's there, not horse or cow or mink. A thing is al- ways what it is, in

spite of what you think A thing is al- ways what it is, in spite of what you think. A

dog's a dog, a cow's a cow, and nei- ther one's a mink."

THE BRAWNY LAD
(Pelagianism)

Once there was a brawn- y lad, who thought he knew it all. Too bad, the thing he did- n't know was, "Pride pre- ceeds a fail." He thought he owned his ver- y self, a- part from God who made him. A

brawn- y   lad   can   do   all   right with- out   the   Lord   to   save him.   So

all   through   life   he   ne- ver knew   that   God's   love   held   him   fast.   Un-

til   one   day,   God's   hand   re- moved,   he   land- ed   on   his

THE 'GATOR
(Psychologism)

When a per- son fol- lows feel- ings, in- stead of what he knows, it's as

though a big ol' 'ga- tor has him firm- ly by the nose.

Pull him this way, pull him that way, pull him all a- round. Since he

does- n't fol- low rea- son, won't he end up up- side down?

THE DO-DO BIRD
(License)

"I am free," said the Do-Do Bird, "free to be bad if I like; To raz-zle and daz-zle, to friz-zle and fraz-zle, no mat-ter if wrong or if right." No won-der you're such a Do-Do bird; not to know what is good in God's

DEAR WORLD
(Hedonism)

Dear world, I want to be hap- py.
Give me mon- ey and plea- sure and fame.
I want it, I want it, I want it, with- out an- y suf- fer- ing or pain.

I WANT MINE
(Individualism)

"I   I want mine," said the wart hog;

"I   I want mine," said the toad.   You can

push the rest a- way   for all I care   and send them

on down the road."   What can you do,   Mis- ter Wart

er, Mis- ter Toad. Think a lit-tle more a- bout the

rest of us, help-ing you and one a- no- ther down the road.

Help- ing you and one a- noth- er down the road. Help- ing

you and one a- noth- er down the road.

Educational Principles

Excerpt from Our Handbook

Catholic schools differ from one another in a variety of ways. All of them exist for spiritual purposes, and all of them aim to provide a good education and discipline in a religious environment. Individual Catholic schools, however, may differ in emphasis. In nineteenth century Africa, for example, Catholic schools were considered works of mercy, promoted by the British Crown when there was no other way for children to learn their ABC's. Inner city schools in America might well emphasize safety, discipline and evangelization. Catholic schools with large enrollments of non-Catholic students might have a special ecumenical flavor.

Ours is a parish school in an area which has many good public schools. Its *primary emphasis*, therefore, is to provide young Catholics--and to a limited extent, other religious children--with a good education *explicitly focussed* on both this life and the next.

Considering not only its primary focus, but also its specific resources and limitations, our school has a very definite idea of what it is and what it is not, what it can accomplish and what it

159

cannot. Parents, therefore, need to be equally clear about their expectations, so that in sending their children here they will not be disappointed.

2. That a school is Catholic from the inside out implies that Catholic beliefs regarding God, human nature and the purpose of life undergird the philosophy and method by which the school operates. In presenting a vision for our school, therefore, we will first discuss the school's foundational Catholic beliefs; then we will speak about the Catholic educational philosophy and methods that we use. In conclusion we will try to describe as clearly as possible, how our school puts these elements together, so that it serves in a specific way. Some of the limitations on our school's resources may leave certain desirable educational objectives beyond its scope. But it is our hope and vision never to be satisfied with present progress, and to do everything we possibly can, to give our children an education that is truly Catholic from the inside out.

3. Before we begin, we would like to remind you that there is no institution in the whole world that has had so much experience in teaching children as the Catholic Church. Think of the very foundation of formal schooling as we know it today: Alcuin at the court of Charlemagne in the eighth century, Robert de Sorbon at the University of Paris in the Middle Ages, the monastic schools and great universities of Europe, the worldwide Jesuit educational system of the Renaissance.

The Catholic Church has its own educational philosophy, tradition and approach. The literature is copious. We have no hesitation, therefore, in setting forth a vision which can tap a 1200-year old tradition of educating children not only for this world but for the next.

I.
Foundational Principles:
Catholic Beliefs Regarding God,
Human Nature and the Purpose of Life

4. Catholic beliefs regarding God, human nature and the purpose of life constitute the very basis and foundation of how Catholic schools operate. For a popular summary of those principles, see the official *Catechism of the Catholic Church.* But here we will list a few highlights, with examples of how they apply to our school's life.

5. *The Trinity.* We are created in the image and likeness of God, Three in One. We are baptized in the name of the Father and of the Son and of the Holy Spirit, into a created share in the relationship of unselfish love which each of the Three has for the others. This unselfish relationship is both pattern for our concept of what we are, and destiny toward which we are called. The ultimate purpose of Catholic education, therefore, is to encourage human growth in that type of unselfish love which the Father, Son, and Holy Spirit have for one another.

6. *Jesus Christ, the Way.* Our way into this Trinitarian life is through Jesus. His words and deeds, attitudes and teachings are to form the norm of how a Catholic school is organized. A school becomes Catholic not so much because it contains good Catholic students or teachers, or because it teaches Catholic doctrine or promotes Catholic religious practices, but because its very life is organized around the teachings and example of Jesus Christ. Another way of saying this is that a Catholic school is a place where children are exposed to Catholic educational culture for seven hours a day, nine months out of the year. Culture means "shared expectations." Not all may agree with all the expectations, nor will all live up to the ideals they presuppose, but no school can be called truly Catholic until it has been made clear, not only in theory but in practice, that there are definite expectations based firmly on gospel principles, about how things in the school are supposed to be.

7. To establish a place where children may experience Catholic educational culture for seven hours a day is the controlling

reason why our parish expends the enormous effort to have a school. To provide such a *setting* for our children is our indirect goal. To impart *knowledge* is our direct goal. (More about this later.)

8. What does it mean that our school is to have a Catholic educational culture? First, it means that we will try to organize the life of our school on the basis of the real Jesus, as taught in Scripture and the tradition of the Catholic Church.

9. The good things which we find in the secular world around us are to be fully affirmed, and the bad things are to be roundly rejected. As a school we make decisions about these things, whether new or old, and that is how we determine the culture of our school. Many examples could be cited. Certainly we affirm academic achievement, good music, the joy of celebrations, healthy sports and the like. But unhealthy elements that come from the world--clothing that makes a cynical statement, music which debases, diabolism, arrogant insolence, disrespect, popular psychologism which excludes humility or exalts self-image into a god, and many more. Because a given practice is popular in today's world does not mean that it is appropriately introduced into the culture of a Catholic school. From the world's point of view, Catholic schools must appear old-fashioned. Our norm and pattern is not popular sentiment, but the teaching and example of Jesus Christ, the way, the truth and the life. For the truly Catholic school, there is no other choice. Additional details in Section II.

10. *The Mass.* Vatican II taught that the Mass is the source and center of the Christian life: "...the liturgy is the summit toward which the activity of the Church is directed; at the same time it is the fountain from which all her power flows."[1] At the Sunday assembly, everything that is good in our lives, including what we do in the school, is brought to the altar, where all is joined to the once-for-all sacrifice of Jesus and offered to the Father. Then from the Mass flows the fountain of power which enables us to serve the Lord in our Catholic school. Thus,

1. Vatican II, *Constitution on the Sacred Liturgy,* n. 10.

participation in Sunday Mass is not something peripheral or optional, but rather central to what we are trying to do. From a perspective of Faith, the Catholic school may be defined as an extension of the Mass; and therefore all Catholics who are part of the school will make it a central priority in their lives. The Mass is celebrated in the midst of a definite community (parish), which is part of the Mystical Body of Christ. Ours is not a disembodied Christ, but one connected to the Catholic Church and its local life. Thus commitment to a particular parish is one of the basic foundations of participation in our Catholic school.

11. *The Primacy of Grace.* The arrogance of secular human-ism claims that the human race has come of age and sooner or later will be able to control the universe. As Catholics, we know different. Jesus said, "Without me you can do nothing" (Jn 15:5). And St. Paul: "I can do all things in Him who strengthens me" (Phil 4:13).

12. We put a lot of human effort into our school, and that includes parents, children, teachers, administrators, parishion-ers. But it is not human effort in which we place our trust. Our trust is in *grace,* that is, God's help in the interior of our souls, urging and inspiring us and giving us strength, and helping us to live out in the setting of our school the life, death and resurrec-tion of the Lord.

13. Grace comes through prayer: daily family prayer at home, public prayer in church, the prayers of our sick people and those who are suffering, prayer before and after each class, activity and meeting. If in eternity we look back on what really happened at our school, and God lets us in on His secrets, we will see a gigantic cosmic battle between the forces of good and the forces of evil, grace and human rebellion, the powers of darkness and the angels of light. Only then will we truly under-stand that our decisive weapon in that battle was grace brought on by prayer. Only then will we understand the words of Jesus, "Fear not; I have overcome the world" (Jn 16:33).

14. *Original Sin.* Secular liberalism assumes that people are so responsible and perfect that any restriction on their liberty is a violation of human dignity. But we Catholics believe in origi-

nal sin, that is, an act of defiance on the part of our first parents, which had serious consequences for the rest of us. After original sin, we remain basically good because created in God's image, but our minds have been darkened and our wills have been weakened so that not only is learning more difficult, but temptations more enticing.   Original sin has many consequences for our school. Here are three examples.

15. First, none of us responsible for the education of children possesses the wisdom we would like to have: neither pastor nor administrators nor teachers nor parents. We live in an imperfect world. We need to be patient with one another. "In many things we all offend (Ja 3:2)."

16. Secondly, learning is not as easy for the children as it would have been had our first parents not sinned. As Newman said, "Knowledge makes a bloody entry into the head." Not all learning will be fun. In today's fallen world, acquiring knowledge requires effort, inner motivation, parental encouragement, discipline, and some pain. The pain in learning is one way that children participate in the mystery of the Christ's cross, which in turn leads them to experience His resurrection.

17. Thirdly, although basically good, all children, because of original sin are inclined to get into mischief. This means that they will need to be corrected, not only for their own good, but for the sake of the scandal they have given to the other children. Jesus was gentle with people. He encouraged the weak and consoled the repentant sinner. But at times he did not hesitate to rebuke them severely, especially when scandal was involved. In a Catholic school, we love children too much to let the risk of their displeasure hold us back from correcting them as needed.

18. *This World and the Next.* Within the one educational process, the Catholic school aims to educate persons as a whole: citizens both of this world and the next.

19. Vatican II clearly stated Catholic teaching on the relationship between the two worlds, heaven and earth: While it profits us nothing if we "gain the whole world and suffer the loss of our own souls (Mt 16:26)," the expectation of reward in the next

world must not weaken, but rather stimulate our concern for this one. In Catholic belief, God uses human achievement, which at the end of the world, He lifts up and uses to create the "new heavens and the new earth."[1] Thus the studies that are needed to educate the human person to make an effective contribution in this world, have their own proper importance and dignity within the Catholic school. Mathematics, language, science, art and music, history, and other appropriate secular subjects are taught there. These subjects will not be isolated from religion, that is, treatment of the religious dimension of art, history, literature and the like, will neither be exaggerated nor minimized. But in the school which is Catholic from the inside out, Faith will clearly appear as the unifying force which gives all these subjects their ultimate meaning. Through them, the Catholic child seeking to grow in the unselfish love which the Father, Son and Holy Spirit have for one another, will find indispensable preparation for service in this world and fulfillment in the next.

II.
Catholic Educational Philosophy
and Educational Method
As Applied to Our School

20. *Progressive Education.* The Catholic educational philosophy and methods which we apply at our school may best be seen in contradistinction to Progressivism,[2] which may be said to constitute the central theory[3] of American public education. Progressivism has its roots in the empirical pragmatism of John Dewey, the self-fulfillment psychology of Sigmund Freud, and the natural child theory of Jean-Jacques Rousseau. As a philosophy of education, it was developed by such educators as Carleton Washburne, William H. Kilpatrick, Harold Rugg, George S.

1. Vatican II, *Church in the Modern World*, n. 39.

2. Lawrence A. Cremin, *Progressivism in American Education* (New York: Vintage, 1964).

3. Progressivism in its completeness never did become the consistent practice in all public school systems. What was widely adopted were bits and pieces in eclectic fashion. See George R. Knight, *Issues and Alternatives in Educational Philosophy*, (Andrews University Press, 1989), p. 87.

Counts, Boyd H. Bode and John L. Childs.

21. As pragmatists, progressives hold that truth is what works. Therefore, they do not see a school primarily as a place where children absorb a set body of knowledge, but as a place where they can experience the kind of cooperative problem-solving that will prepare them to live as good citizens in a democracy.[1] Progressives do not reject the teaching of content, but they favor a curriculum that grows out of the student's needs, interests and intuitions.[2] Their method of teaching leans more toward the experiential and informal,[3] rather than the traditional formal methods involving heavy reliance on text-books, drill, memorization and competition. For Progressives, the teacher is more of a guide and enabler rather than one who transmits a body of knowledge to the student with authority.

22. The focus of progressive education is on learning skills and moral behavior that will make democracy work.[4] As a follower of Hume and other British empiricists who maintained that nothing could be affirmed unless scientifically proven, Dewey taught that moral behavior could not be validated by belief in God. The only possible foundation for moral behavior is the pragmatic one that moral behavior makes life in a democracy work.[5] This idea had enormous influence on progressive education, which accepted the pragmatic usefulness of the second great commandment, love of neighbor, but dismissed the

1. John Dewey, *The School and Society*, originally published 1956 (University of Chicago Press, 1990).

2. John Dewey, "The Child and the Curriculum," in Steven M. Cahn, ed., *Classic and Contemporary Readings in the Philosophy of Education* (McGraw-Hill, 1997). This essay was first published in 1902.

3. John Dewey, "Experience and Education," in Steven M. Cahn, *Classic and Contemporary Readings in the Philosophy of Education* (McGraw-Hill, 1007), pp. 000 ff. Examples of the experiential method would be field trips and group projects.

4. John Dewey, *Democracy and Education: An Introduction to the Philosophy of Education* (Free Press, 1916).

5. John Dewey, *Moral Principles in Education*, (Southern Illinois University Press, 1909).

love, adoration and worship of God, which is the first.

23. Finally, Progressives look to the school to change moral behavior in the interest of solving social ills. Thus the tendency of progressive education to bypass parents and church, and see itself as the principal agent of teaching behavior and effecting moral reform.

Traditional Catholic
Philosophy of Education

24. While Catholic philosophers affirm some of the insights of progressive education, their emphasis is entirely different.[1] In the Catholic view, education guides human persons in the evolving process whereby they shape themselves, with the help of grace, as children of God, armed with the knowledge, strength of judgment and moral virtues that they need as citizens of this world and the next.[2] Not all education takes place in the school. In Catholic tradition, parents, assisted by the Church, have primary responsibility for their children's education.[3] The school does not usurp the role of parents, but rather provides them with a very specific help in their task: *the training of the child's intellect and memory, and the imparting of knowledge.*[4] It is this knowledge which children will need to help them live successfully as citizens of this world and the next.

25. The school also offers help in children's moral development,[5] even though moral development is not the school's primary focus. It does this by imparting knowledge about morality and its foundations in Christian belief, by expecting moral behavior of the child as a participant in the school

---

1. See, for example, Jacques Maritain, *Education at the Crossroads*, (Yale University Press, 1943), p. 16.

2. Vatican II, *Declaration on Christian Education*, n. 2.

3. *Ibid.,,* n. 3.

4. *Ibid.,* n. 5.

5. *Ibid.,,* n. 8.

community, by so organizing the school that the child experiences a Christian educational culture for several hours a day, and by giving witness of Christian discipleship and good example.

26. The imparting of knowledge, through instruction on the part of teachers, and study on the part of students,[1] is viewed as a pursuit of and delight in truth. In Catholic philosophy, *truth* is not considered to be "what works," but a correspondence between the mind and the objective reality.[2] The truth may come through divine revelation, or through human observation or experience. There can be no contradiction between the two, because both are one in the sight of God. According to the Aristotelian-Thomistic tradition of modified realism,[3] we do not merely know our *ideas* of things, as modern subjectivism would hold, but we grasp things *as they are in themselves,* even though not perfectly, because of human limitations.[4]

Catholics believe in the existence of a stable, objective body of truth, known through divine revelation as well as through human reason and science. Believing that learning this body of truth is important for the child's education, Catholics have traditionally placed the acquisition of knowledge and the training of the intellect and memory at the center of schooling. It is understandable why Progressives, with their pessimism about the very existence of a stable[5] body of knowledge beyond the empirical, would desire to shift the educational emphasis of the school to the child and his subjective perceptions and feelings. This is certainly consonant with the subjectivist philosophies characteristic of our times. But we do not accept the Progressivist educational

1. Thomas Aquinas, *Summa Theologica*, II-II, Q. 166, Art. 1.

2. Aquinas, *Summa Theologica*, I, Q. 85, Art. 6.

3. Francis J. Selman, *St. Thomas Aquinas: Teacher of Truth*, (Edinburgh: T Clark, 1994).

4. Aquinas, *Summa Theologica*, I, Q. 85, Art. 2.

5. A typical statement of the philosopical position of many Progressives may be found in Alfred North Whitehead's essay, "The Aims of Education," in Cahn, *Readings*, pp. 261 ff.

emphasis, or the philosophy upon which it is based, as a suitable focus for a Catholic school.

27. The learning that occurs will not be confined to religious subjects, but will embrace secular subjects as well. In Catholic thought, religion provides the unifying force for all knowledge, but secular knowledge has its proper place. Thus children study mathematics in order to prepare themselves for their role in building up the world,[1] so that God can on the last day elevate their accomplishments to become part of the new heavens and the new earth. Mathematics, therefore is important, not just because it will enable children to earn a lot of money as adults, or because it will make democracy work, but because it will prepare them to build up God's world and improve on the arrangement of creation, while simultaneously providing a living to maintain themselves and their families in frugal comfort.

28. *The children to be educated* are to be viewed in Christian terms: they are created in the image of the Triune God, weakened by original sin, redeemed by Christ, born again in baptism, and aided by grace within family and Church. They are destined through the cross and resurrection of Jesus the Way, to attain a created share in the inner life of the Father, Son and Holy Spirit, in this life and in the life to come.

29. *The ideal teacher* in the Catholic system is struggling to enter as deeply as possible into a created share in the life of the Father, Son and Holy Spirit, as given in baptism. This means that teachers, although wounded by original sin like everyone else, are trying, with God's grace to be loving persons after the example of Jesus Christ. As educators, they are first to be contemplative scholars, active agents of learning, experts in their subjects, skillful teachers and lovers of truth. St. Thomas Aquinas describes the teacher as one who overflows with love of truth, and shares that overflow with others.[2] Thus in Catholic philosophy the teacher is not just a guide and enabler, but a

---

1. Vatican II, *Education*, n. 2.

2. Aquinas, *Summa Theologica*, II-II, Q. 181, Art. 3.

leader and an active agent.

From a secular perspective, our teachers are employees subject to civil taxes and the like; but from a religious perspective they are Ministers of Catholic Schooling. They are semi-volunteers, since they do not--nor are they likely to--receive compensation comparable to teachers in the public school system. Their willingness to serve as semi-volunteer constitutes part of the endowment of the school. Our teachers are here because (1) they believe in our philosophy of education, (2) they desire to serve Jesus as Ministers of Schooling in accordance with that philosophy; and (3) they are at that point in their lives where their family obligations permit them to serve as semi-volunteers on the compensation we offer.

30. *The ultimate motivation for learning* that is offered to the child, is the opportunity of sharing in the life, death and resurrection of Jesus, as a way into the inner life of the Father, Son and Holy Spirit. Through the Mass, children are privileged to stand before God's altar and offer their efforts to learn, painful as they sometimes are, to the Father's glory. But in imitation of Jesus, who offered people not only this ultimate motivation, but the secondary motivation of heaven (and hell) as well, students in the Catholic system are offered the secondary motivation of earthly recognition and praise, and other moderate and simple material rewards, for their achievements as they grow in wisdom and knowledge before God and men. Because of original sin, the negative motivation of moderate punishment also has its place.[1]

31. Catholic educational philosophy is open to a variety of *modern approaches and teaching methods*, as long as they are compatible with its aims. For example, we accept the valid insights of such thinkers as Komensky, Dewey, Erikson and Piaget about the need to relate learning to children's level of development, but we reject the false inference that "You cannot teach children anything they do not want to learn." Nor do we believe that the decision about what should be learned is to be

---

1. See section on original sin, n. 14 above.

left largely in the children's hands, to the detriment of the heritage of the past. We see the value of a certain amount of informal, experiential methodology in the school, provided the teacher insures that learning actually occurs. But we would not want overemphasis on this method to diminish the quantity of systematic knowledge that the student needs to attain.[1] In general, we will be open to new methods, but slow to adopt them. Careful discernment is needed before new educational approaches will be introduced, especially when the underlying assumptions seem to be coming from a pragmatist or subjectivist philosophical direction.

32. Finally, Catholic educational philosophy affirms the legitimacy of testing and rewarding the knowledge actually attained.

III.
The Specific Functions of Our School

33. In light of all this, the specific purpose and function of our school can be described as follows.

34. The primary function of our school is to assist parents in seeing that their children obtain the *elementary knowledge* which they need as citizens of this world and the next. We test and gives public recognition to this knowledge, to insure that learning actually takes place. Learning is the direct goal of our school.

35. The indirect goal of our school is to provide a setting for Christian growth. Some ways it does this is by teaching children about morality and its foundations; by expecting moral behavior of the child at school; by so organizing the school that the child experiences, for several hours a day, an educational

---

1. The Fourth General Assembly of the Synod of Bishops called for "the restoration of a judicious balance between reflection and spontaneity, between dialogue and silence, between written work and memory work." *Catechesi Tradendae*, October 16, 1979. See also: *The National Catechetical Directory for Catholics of the United States* (NCCB, 1977), p. 176.

culture that is Catholic; by giving witness of Christian discipleship through the way teachers, staff and students relate to one
another; by offering retreats, and by providing opportunities for
Sacraments, prayer and religious devotions in the school context. In addition, the school can call on the parish to offer liturgical and devotional experiences to students, as well as whatever
training parents might need and request for enhancing their own
skills in guiding their children's intellectual, moral and spiritual
development.

36. The *parents* whom the school assists are parishioners
committed enough in their relationship with Jesus that they (or
covenanted sponsors provided by them) give their children good
example by weekly attendance at our parish Sunday Mass.
(Children of other parishes and of other faiths, whose parents
are faithful to their religious duties in their church of registration, are admitted to our school as honored guests.)

37. As a parish school, we serve *children with a wide range
of educational capacities.* They will be within the range that
can be taught successfully by one teacher in a heterogeneous
(mixed) classroom grouping, with the help of specialized services which the government provides. We are neither an academy nor a remedial school; we do not favor one end of the spec-
trum over the other. We do not have the resources to work with
children who have deep psychological problems, or whose
behavior is disruptive or gives scandal, or who have a fragile
self-image, or who are not faithful to their Sunday Mass and
other religious obligations.

38. By *elementary knowledge*, we mean the academic learning that will provide the basis for later liberal, vocational or
technical studies, and for higher specialized fields. This includes: the elements of grammar, how to read with comprehension, how to spell, how to write coherent sentences and paragraphs, basic mathematical skills, the elements of music and art,
introduction to science, how to use libraries and computers,
basic social studies, and foundations of the Catholic Faith. With
the exception of retreats, Sacraments, devotions, student leadership council and physical education, the school itself does not
provide for children's non-academic needs. Nevertheless, a

great variety of opportunities for well-rounded development is furnished through the parish: sports, Scouts, leadership training, volunteer service opportunities, social activities, choir, and drama. Additional opportunities are available in the community.

39. It is our determination never to be satisfied with present progress, and to do everything we possibly can to enlarge our vision and deepen our commitment to making our school truly Catholic from the inside out.

Catholic Writings We Consulted

BUETOW, Harold A. *The Catholic School: Its Roots, Identity, and Future*. Crossroad, 1988.

----------. *Of Singular Benefit: The Story of Catholic Education in the United States*. Macmillan, 1970.

BYRNES, James T. *John Paul II and Educating for Life: Moving Toward a Renewal of Catholic Educational Philosophy*. Peter Lang, 2002.

CONWAY, Pierre H. *Principles of Education: A Thomistic Approach*. Thomist Press, 1960.

COOK, Timothy J. *Architects of Catholic Culture: Designing & Building Catholic Culture in Catholic Schools*. NCEA, 2001.

CRONIN, Patricia H. *Character Development in the Catholic School*. NCEA, 1999.

CUNNINGHAM, William F. *The Pivotal Problems of Education: An Introduction to the Christian Philosophy of Education.* Macmillan, 1940.

CURTIS, Sarah A. *Educating the Faithful: Religion, Schooling and Society in Nineteenth-Century France.* Northern Illinois University, 2000.

D'SOUZA, Mario O. "Maritain's Philosophy of Education and Christian Religious Education," *Catholic Education* (4:3, 2001).

----------. "Maritain's Seven Misconceptions of Education," *Catholic Education* (5:4, 2002).

DeHOVRE, Franz. *Philosophy and Education.* Benziger, 1931.

----------. *Catholicism in Education.* Benziger, 1934.

DONLAN, Thomas.*Theology and Education.* Brown, 1952.

DOUGHERTY, Jude P. *Recent American Naturalism: An Exposition and Critique.* Catholic University, 1960.

FITZPATRICK, Edward A. *Philosophy of Education.* Bruce, 1953.

----------. *LaSalle: Patron of All Teachers.* Bruce, 1951.

FLUSCHE, Ernest A. *A Critical Study of Current Concepts of Truth in American Educational Theory and Their Educational Implications.* Catholic University Press, 1961.

FULLER, Edmund, ed. *The Christian Idea of Education: Papers and Discussions.* Yale University, 1957.

GALLAGHER, Donald and Idella. *The Educational Philosophy of Jacques Maritain.* Doubleday, 1962.

GLEASON, P. *What Made Catholic Identity a Problem*. University of Dayton, 1994.

GROOME, Thomas. *Educating for Life: A Spiritual Vision for Every Teacher and Parent*. Thomas More, 1998.

GUISSANI, Luigi. *The Risk of Education: Discovering Our Ultimate Destiny*. Crossroad, 1995.

GULLEY, Anthony D. *A Philosophical Study of the Efficient Causes of Learning According to St. Thomas Aquinas*. Catholic University Press, 1961.

JOHNSON, George. "The Need for a Catholic Philosophy of Education," in Charles A. Hart., ed., *Aspects of the New Scholastic Philosophy*. Benziger, 1932.

JOHNSTON, Herbert. *A Philosophy of Education*. McGraw Hill, 1963.

KANE, William T. *Some Principles of Education*. Loyola University, 1938.

KELLY, Francis D. *The Mystery We Proclaim: Catechesis at the Third Millennium*. Our Sunday Visitor, 1993.

LEEN, Edward. *What Is Education?* Sheed & Ward, 1944.

LONERGAN, Bernard. *Topics in Education*, Volume 10 of *The Collected Works of Bernard Lonergan*. University of Toronto, 1988.

LUZBETAK, Louis J., *The Church and Culture: New Perspectives in Missiological Anthropology* (Orbis, 1988.

MCCLUSKEY, Neil G. *Catholic Viewpoint on Education*. Doubleday, 1962.

MCDERMOTT, Edwin J. *Distinctive Qualities of the Catholic School*. NCEA, 1997.

MCGLADE, Joseph.*Progressive Educators and the Catholic Church*. Newman Press, 1953.

MCGUCKEN, William J. *The Catholic Way in Education*. Loyola University Press, 1962.

MCINERNY, Daniel, ed. *The Common Things: Essays on Thomism and Education*. American Maritain Association, 1999.

MARIQUE, Pierre.*The Philosophy of Christian Education*. Prentice-Hall, 1939.

MARITAIN, Jacques.*Education at the Crossroads*. Yale University Press, 1943.

MAYER, Mary H. *The Philosophy of Teaching of St. Thomas Aquinas*. Bruce, 1929.

MORRISON, John. *The Educational Philosophy of St. John Bosco*. Salesian Publications, 1979.

O'BRIEN, Kevin J. *The Proximate Aim of Education: A Study of the Proper and Immediate End of Education*. Catholic University Press, 1958.

O'HARA, James H. *Limitations of the Educational Theory of John Dewey*. Catholic University Press, 1929.

O'NEILL, Michael.*New Schools in a New Church: Toward a Modern Philosophy of Catholic Education*. St. John's University Press, 1971.

REDDEN, John D. and Francis A. Ryan. *A Catholic Philosophy of Education*. Bruce, 1956.

REDPATH, Peter A., ed. *From Twilight to Dawn: The Cultural Vision of Jacques Maritain*. Notre Dame, 1990.

REITZ, Donald J. *Moral Crisis in the Schools: What Parents and Teachers Need to Know*. Cathedral, 1998.

SCANLAN, Michael. *Let the Fire Fall.* Franciscan University of Steubenville, 1997.

SCHULER, Paul. *Reaction of American Catholics to the Foundations and Early Practices of Progressive Education in the United States 1892-1917.* Doctoral dissertation, Notre Dame, 1970.

SHIELDS, Thomas Edward.*Philosophy of Education: Lectures.* Catholic Education Press, 1917.

SPALDING, J. L. *Means and Ends of Education.* McClurg, 1909.

SPANGLER, Mary M. *Principles of Education: A Study of Aristotelian Thomism Contrasted with Other Philosophies.* University Press of America, 1983.

TUOHY, John W. *The De Magistro of St. Augustine and the De Magistro of St. Thomas Aquinas Compared.* Catholic University Press, 1937.

VAN GRIEKEN, George A. *Touching the Hearts of Students: Characteristics of Lasallian Schools.* Christian Brothers, 1999.

WELCH, Mary Leanne. *Methods of Teaching in the Catholic School.* NCEA, 1987.

WALCH, Timothy. *Parish School: American Catholic Parochial Education from Colonial Times to the Present.* Crossroad, 1996.

WARD, L. *Philosophy of Education.* Regnery, 1963.

YOUNISS, James, John J. Convey, and Jeffrey A. McClellan, eds., *The Catholic Character of Catholic Schools.* Notre Dame, 2000.

CHURCH DOCUMENTS

PIUS XI. *The Christian Education of Youth, Rappresentanti in Terra 1929.*

VATICAN II. *Declaration on Christian Education, Gravissimum Educationis 1965.*

SACRED CONGREGATION FOR THE CLERGY. *General Catechetical Directory 1997.*

NATIONAL CONFERENCE OF CATHOLIC BISHOPS. *To Teach as Jesus Did: A Pastoral Message on Catholic Education 1972.*

NATIONAL CONFERENCE OF CATHOLIC BISHOPS. *Sharing the Light of Faith: National Catechetical Directory for Catholics of the United States 1978.*

JOHN PAUL II. *Catechesi Tradendae. Catechesis in Our Time 1979.*

SACRED CONGREGATION FOR CATHOLIC EDUCATION. *The Catholic School 1977.*

----------. *Lay Catholics in Schools: Witnesses to Faith 1982.*

----------. *The Religious Dimension of Education in a Catholic School 1988.*

----------. *The Catholic School on the Threshold of the Third Millennium 1997.*

BIBLIOGRAPHY

HUNT, Thomas C., Ellis A. Joseph and Ronald J. Nuzzi, eds., *Catholic Schools Still Make a Difference: Ten Years of Research 1991-2000.* NCEA, 2002.

----------. *Handbook of Research on Catholic Education.*

Greenwood, 2001.

YOUNISS, James and John J. Convey. *Catholic Schools at the Crossroads: Survival and Transformation.* Teachers College Press, 2000.

HUNT, Thomas C. *Doctoral Dissertations on Catholic Schools in the United States 1988-1997.* National Center for Research in Catholic Education, NCEA 1998.

CONVEY, John J. *Catholic Schools Make a Difference: Twenty-five Years of Research* (1965-1991). NCEA.

TRAVIS, Mary Peter. *Doctoral Dissertations on Catholic Schools, K-12 1976-1987.* National Center for Research in Total Catholic Education, NCEA 1989.

JOURNALS

Catholic Education: A Journal of Inquiry and Practice addresses many of the issues in which we are interested, as well as providing a guide to new literature. This journal, founded by Fordham University, St. Louis University, The University of Dayton, and The University of San Francisco, includes among its goals "drawing upon the philosophical and theological traditions of Catholic education, as well as an interdisciplinary perspective, in analyzing these issues."

Momentum is the official journal of the National Catholic Educational Association.

Index

181